mod knots

Creating Jewelry & Accessories with Macramé

Cathi Milligan

NORTH LIGHT BOOKS

Cincinnati, Ohio

www.mycraftivity.com

13 12 11 10 09   5 4 3 2 1

Distributed in Canada by Fraser Direct
100 Armstrong Avenue
Georgetown, ON, Canada L7G 5S4
Tel: (905) 877-4411

Distributed in the U.K. and Europe by David & Charles
Brunel House, Newton Abbot, Devon, TQ12 4PU, England
Tel: (+44) 1626 323200, Fax: (+44) 1626 323319
E-mail: postmaster@davidandcharles.co.uk

Distributed in Australia by Capricorn Link
P.O. Box 704, S. Windsor, NSW 2756 Australia
Tel: (02) 4577-3555

Library of Congress Cataloging-in-Publication Data

Milligan, Cathi.
   Mod knots : creating jewelry and accessories with macramé / by Cathi Milligan. -- 1st ed.
        p. cm.
   Includes index.
   ISBN 978-1-60061-144-5 (pbk. : alk. paper)
   1. Macramé. 2. Jewelry making. I. Title.
   TT840.M33M45 2009
   746.42'22--dc22

2008037483

Editor: Jessica Strawser
Designer: Corrie Shaffeld
Photographers: Christine Polomsky,
Ric Deliantoni and Al Parrish
Stylist: Nora Martini
Production Coordinator: Greg Nock

www.fwmedia.com

Metric Conversion Chart

to convert	to	multiply by
Inches	Centimeters	2.54
Centimeters	Inches	0.4
Feet	Centimeters	30.5
Centimeters	Feet	0.03
Yards	Meters	0.9
Meters	Yards	1.1
Sq. Inches	Sq. Centimeters	6.45
Sq. Centimeters	Sq. Inches	0.16
Sq. Feet	Sq. Meters	0.09
Sq. Meters	Sq. Feet	10.8
Sq. Yards	Sq. Meters	0.8
Sq. Meters	Sq. Yards	1.2
Pounds	Kilograms	0.45
Kilograms	Pounds	2.2
Ounces	Grams	28.3
Grams	Ounces	0.035

DEDICATION

This goes out to my Mom, Desiree, a.k.a. Dee Dee. Thanks for all of your support!

ACKNOWLEDGMENTS

My original exposure to macramé and beads comes from hanging out at a bead store, Macraménia, in my early teen years. Without this store, I wouldn't know about the wonderful and beautiful jewelry and accessories that could be created with macramé. Thanks, Suzanne Miller.

I'm very grateful to everyone over at the San Gabriel Bead Company, Kelly especially, for helping me get so many of my macramé supplies. And the ladies over at The Stitch Café were so immensely helpful with my exploration into new materials. I'm a bit jealous of knitters.

My production team at F+W is awesome. I couldn't have had more fun with my editor, Jessica Strawser, and photographer, Christine Polomsky, during my photo shoot. Also thanks to Tonia Davenport for all her assistance.

A giant thanks goes to my man, Jack, for putting up with almost nonstop talk about macramé and beads. Yarn and leather lace and beads all over the place, projects everywhere. It's all for the sake of the macramé!

CONTENTS

INTRODUCTION

When most people think of macramé, they picture hippies and plant hangers and even have memories of summer camp, where they were first exposed to the art of knotting, also known as macramé. They say, "Oh I remember macramé. I did that when I was young," or, "My mom used to do that." Well, macramé is more than that—a lot more than that.

Macramé has been around for many, many centuries. The art of knotting first originated in the Middle East as a means of making nets and decorating the edges of fabric. Sailors created these in their travels, and through travel, trade and the conquering of distant lands, macramé spread across the world. It had its heyday in the Victorian ages when the craft was widely regarded. Today most people remember macramé from the 1970s, but that was far from the beginning.

My goal in creating *Mod Knots* was to upend what is most associated with macramé. I'll start by teaching you all the basic knots, step by step, and I'll introduce you to the most commonly used materials, such as hemp, linen and nylon cord—and then to some not so common ones, including handspun yarn, soft leather lace and even wire. Then we'll begin making jewelry that you may never have imagined you could achieve with macramé. In making one-of-a-kind necklaces, bracelets, earrings and even jewelry sets, we'll combine materials in unexpected ways and blend macramé with a variety of other jewelry-making techniques, such as wire wrapping, bead stringing, and even metal clay and leatherwork. We'll also make accessories, such as belts and handbags and even a guitar strap, as well as a couple of wearables, including a halter-top and a soft variegated wool scarf. So cute! And it's not your mother's macramé. I hope these new explorations in macramé will inspire your own future adventures with this versatile (and fun!) craft.

MATERIALS

Macramés utilitarian beginnings were with jute, hemp and linen, as well as other fibers that were mostly used for nets and fabric. As sailors and traders obtained different types of material from the lands they ventured to, they helped to develop the craft—and to pass it on, too.

Fast-forward to the present day, where we have new technologies, materials and, of course, the Internet, and you have the most amazing array of fibers and beads and findings to create just about anything you can imagine.

Macramé requires more that just fiber, beads and findings, though. Many of the tools you'll need to create the projects in this book you probably already own. Anything you don't have on hand can be easily acquired at your local bead or craft store or, in some cases, even your local hardware store.

Macramé Boards

Macramé projects need to be mounted—usually with T pins and/or masking tape—to a surface as you work. This makes working with your cords easier and helps keep the knots tight and neatly aligned. Specially designed macramé boards are available at your local bead or craft store, or through online retailers, and work for most projects. They typically measure approximately 12" × 18" (30cm × 46cm) and are made from fiberboard. Most manufactured macramé boards have a grid on the surface as well as rulers along the sides. They can be removed, but I leave them shrink-wrapped or taped into place, as I find them very helpful guides as I work. Some even include instructional illustrations of the basic macramé knots.

If your project is too large to fit on a standard macramé board, you may have to make your own. Choose a porous surface that you can easily pin your work to. You'll also want to select a surface that you can repeatedly adhere, remove and reposition tape to easily and without

damage. For wider projects, I've used the surface of an old desk. For a long curtain, I once built a 3' × 6' (91cm × 183cm) wooden board to get the job done. If you do end up making your own macrame surface, you'll want to draw a grid on it and add rulers to the sides. If you're working on an unorthodox surface, like a table or airplane tray, you may even want to add a piece of tape with measurements marked on it so you have a reference close at hand.

Pins and Tape

Pins are used to secure your project to your macramé board so it doesn't move around as you work. They also come in handy for holding certain strands in place as you incorporate various knot sequences and other design elements into your projects.

T-pins are the most popular choice for macramé. They have a nice length, and their shape makes them easy to insert and remove repeatedly. Ball-end pins used for sewing can also be used, but they're not quite as sturdy as T-pins. Avoid substitut-

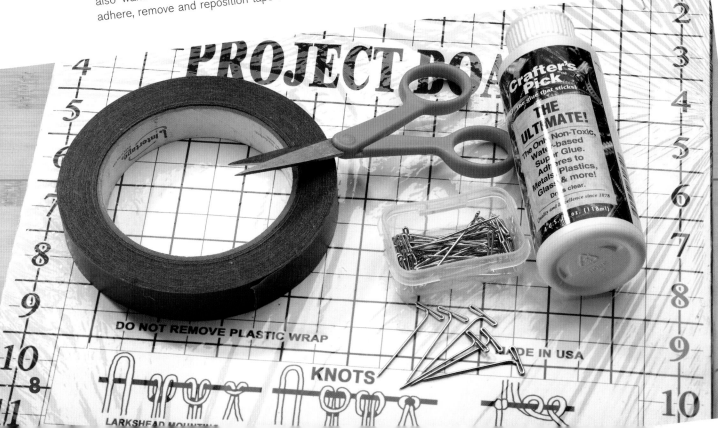

ing push pins and thumb tacks, both of which tend to be too short.

Masking tape is also used to secure materials to your work surface. It can be a substitute for T-pins if you're working on a more delicate surface, but it's most often used to secure "filler cords"—or cords that you're tying your working cords around—while tying square and twist knots. (You'll learn more about these on the following pages.) I prefer the blue painter's masking tape, as it tends to be easier to remove and reposition as you work than regular masking tape. Avoid substituting duct tape, packing tape or any other clear tape; they're all too sticky and can damage your cords and your surface and be all-around difficult to remove.

Scissors

Most macramé projects are made with thin fibers that are easy to cut with a standard pair of craft scissors like those you probably already own. To trim the excess length when a project is complete, you may want to get a pair of little trimming scissors designed for sewing. They'll allow you to get really close to any knot where you want to trim.

Some of the projects in this book use suede and leather hide and cord. Those require a more powerful pair of scissors to cut. There are wonderful economy scissors from the leather store that have become my favorite all-around perfect scissors. They can handle the hides, yet are small enough to trim ends close to knots, and they're great for just about everything else. If you plan to work with these materials frequently, it's worth the investment to get a higher quality pair of scissors.

Adhesives

Most macramé projects are completed by securing the final knot(s) with adhesive. The type of adhesive to use will depend on the materials being used. White glue is great for waxed linen, hemp, cotton, silk and other fibers. Rubber cement or contact cement is best suited for leather and suede. E-6000 and epoxy are very strong adhesives that are used for gluing nonporous objects together, such as wire and even the labradorite beads that are used with the heart belt buckle on page 86. Both of these adhesives do require proper ventilation during use, and all warning labels should be strictly followed. My personal favorite is The Ultimate!, a nontoxic, water-based super glue that is really strong and flexible. When deciding which adhesive is best to use for your project, do keep in mind the toxicity of the glue, especially if it's going to come in contact with skin.

Cords

If you can tie a knot in it, you can probably macramé with it. **Waxed-linen and waxed hemp** are two of the more popular types of fiber to work with. Both are available in a wide array of colors and thicknesses. The wax coating on these cords makes them hold a knot exceptionally well. Your knots and your resulting knot patterns will be well defined. Bead and craft stores carry these cords, or you can easily find them online.

Another popular material to macramé with is **rattail**, a satin cord that comes in a rainbow of colors and at least three different thicknesses. Rattail was popular in the 1970s but has never gone out of style with crafters who like to incorporate Chinese Knots or Celtic Knots into their work. It can be slippery, so knots tied in rattail can loosen if not secured well. But the results look so beautiful that this material is really worth using.

Polypropylene or polyolefin cord is another long-standing favorite. It's used to make rope for boating, hauling and any vocation that requires a very strong, durable material that is also waterproof. It's also great for purses, hammocks or even the collar and leash project on page 98. The color selection isn't that great, but the utilitarian properties make it a good choice for certain projects. You can find it at your local hardware store.

Leather and suede lace are great macramé materials. There are a number of weights of laces available. Look for the more soft and supple laces, and avoid stiffer versions that may be difficult to tie. When deciding which type of hide to use, consider the form and function of your project. Is it a purse? A belt? Should the material be rugged and ready to take a beating, or will it be treated more delicately? There's a delicate, soft suede I've used for small bags, a beaded curtain and even a necklace, but I know from experience that a larger bag would require a thicker and sturdier lace. An alternative to leather and suede is ultra-suede. **Ultra-suede** is a synthetic fabric that has a very similar feel to suede but is machine washable and resists stains. It is available in a wide array of colors and a few different thicknesses. Countless varieties, styles and colors of leather, suede and ultra-suede are available at your local bead, craft or leather store, as well as online.

Cotton and wool yarns are used in several of the accessories in this book, including a scarf, a purse and even a halter top. There are so many gorgeous yarns out there, and I have to admit, I've always been a bit jealous of knitters and all their options! But I don't want to knit. I do, however, want the yarn. When you go to the yarn store, experiment with your choices. In addition to ordinary cotton and wool blends, you'll find varying textures in bamboo yarn, cashmere, alpaca, angora and more. Chunky, variegated yarns (like the one I used for the scarf on page 112) are my favorites. Indulge in luscious, hand-dyed fibers.

The main things to consider when deciding what type of yarn to work with: How well does it knot? If the material is too slippery the knot can fall out. Will you have enough material? In the case of some specialty yarns, what they have in stock may be all they can get. I learned this the hard way with a purse I was working on. I bought only two skeins of the yarn, even though they had three. When I was mounting the yarn to the handles, I used one skein per handle and found I didn't have enough yarn to complete the project. Of course the last skein had been sold. Oops. I was able to get a nice, neutral cotton that matched to fill in, but I sure did learn a lesson that day. Sometimes it's better to buy all of that special color to ensure you'll have enough materials. It's better to have extra rather than not enough.

Wire

Wire is a difficult material to use for macramé—but if you master the art, the results can be amazingly unique jewelry pieces. The nature of metal is not to bend repeatedly. It lacks flexibility and repeated bending causes wire to become work-hardened and brittle. It will eventually break if you bend it back and forth over and over. Also, heavier wire doesn't like to bend without an incredible amount of effort. Most macramé with metal is done with thinner

Within this book, we use semiprecious gemstones, pearls, vintage seed beads, new seed beads, handmade lampwork glass beads, metal beads, bone beads and even sometimes buttons. They come in all shapes, hues and sizes.

In searching for the beads you'll use in your project, one of the most important considerations is the size of their holes. Each bead has to be able to accommodate the materials you're planning to knot with. If you can't thread your material through the bead's hole, the hole has to be enlarged—likely more work than you're willing to do. You may want to bring a sample of the material that you are planning to use with you to the bead or craft store. Alternatively, the variation in the wire wrap project on page 56 offers up a more innovative solution for big bead-small hole problems. If you find yourself with a bunch of beads that have holes so small they seem completely useless, you can use them for the belt buckle in the leather belt project on page 86.

Hardware and Findings

These purely functional materials might not be as fun to select, but they're still necessary. Jewelry findings include clasps and earring wires (unless, that is, you want to make your own; see page 26). They are available at your local bead and craft stores as well as many online retailers.

For accessories, other hardware may be necessary. Fabric stores, craft and hardware stores and even leather stores are good sources for belt buckles, clips and metal rings. Purse handles can be found through a number of sources, from craft stores to knitting and fabric stores. There are ridged handles made from plastic, metal and bamboo (like the pair used in the purse on page 116). Leather and leather-like handles offer more flexible options. And again, most of these items can also be found online.

gauge wire, which is easier to manipulate. It will still stiffen when worked, so the less you bend it the better.

The wire used most in this book is sterling silver. If you haven't worked with wire before, you may want to become more familiar with it by using a less expensive metal wire first. There are many types of wire to choose from, such as brass, copper and art wire that come in a bunch of different colors. Most of these wires are available in a variety of thicknesses, also known as gauges. The lower the gauge number is, the thicker the wire is. To make a clasp, 20g to 16g works best. 14g wire is difficult to bend due to its thickness. I find 26g to 22g best for macramé. To use a thicker gauge is too difficult and the wire generally ends up with too many tool marks and kinks. Opt for softer varieties whenever you can. You'll learn more about working with wire on page 25.

Beads

Most macramé projects wouldn't be complete without beads. (I think life itself wouldn't be complete without beads, but that's just me; I happen to also make glass beads in addition to my macramé skills.) The bead options available are staggering. When I first learned how to macramé, the selection of beads to work with was limited. Bead storeowners usually had to travel to obtain the interesting beads they offered. Since trade around the world has opened, as well as the developments in technology, the beads that jewelry designers have to choose from today is almost overwhelming.

tip

Whenever I'm out in my travels and I find myself at a thrift store, I always check the purses and belts for interesting handles and buckles. You never know what you may find or what may inspire you.

TOOLS

Macramé itself doesn't require much in the way of tools, but the other techniques included in this book do. Here's a list of the tools that will be required to complete some of the projects:

Jewelry hammer and a bench block or anvil
The two items are used in conjunction with one another; the hammer is used to strike the surface of the metal and the anvil or bench block is used to support the metal being struck or forged. The anvil or bench block is made of hardened steel that can withstand the impacts it receives.

Round-nose pliers
Used primarily for jewelry making due to its ability to form wire into nice curves and loops, since the jaws are round and taper to a point.

Chain-nose pliers
Sometime called needle-nose pliers, these are also used a lot in jewelry making to assist in opening jump rings or earring wires or to bend or hold wire.

Wire cutters
A hand tool used to clip off the ends of wire.

Crimping pliers
A specific type of pliers used in conjunction with crimp beads and beading wire that compresses the crimp bead to secure the beading wire and the beads or findings.

Soft Flex beading wire
A brand of beading wire that is made up of 49 tiny strands of steel that is encased with a plastic coating. This type of material is made by other manufacturers too and is used with crimp beads to secure everything.

Crimp beads
A type of bead that is used with beading wire to secure the beads and findings that is compressed or crimped.

Wood dowel
It's a long piece of rounded wood that is available in a variety of thicknesses and lengths. Dowels have a number of uses and in this case it's used to assist in shaping wire.

Silver/black patina solution
This patina material, which darkens the surface of silver, using a little bit of acids and nasty chemicals, should be treated with the utmost care.

Steel wool
A small mass made up of thin fibers of steel that's abrasive quality is the only thing that effectively removes the dark patina created by the silver/black patina solution.

Leather hole punch
This leather-working tool has a wheel with a variety of sizes to punch many hole sizes into leather or suede.

Soldering block and tripod
The tripod provides a raised surface to place the fireproof soldering block on to solder and be able to work in a safer situation.

Butane torch
A small handheld torch that provides sufficient fire and heat to solder small silver items or fire metal clay.

Butane
The fuel used for butane torches.

Dremel or other rotary tool
A multi-tasking tool that comes with attachments to buff, polish, grind and drill, among other things, the materials you're working with.

Toaster oven
Polymer clay requires baking to cure it and the toaster oven is perfect for that task, providing the right heat. Once used with polymer clay, the toaster oven should not be used for food.

Plastic bobbins
These assist in controlling extra long pieces of macramé material, making them easier to knot, by winding the material onto the bobbin and closing it around it, encapsulating the material inside and keeping it manageable.

The tools and supplies are available through your local hardware, craft or bead stores. If you can't find what you need, check online. The resources list on page 124 should help you locate many of the items listed.

MACRAMÉ TECHNIQUES

Macramé is a crafting technique built from a variety of different knots that create patterns and designs. There aren't many knots, but the numerous design variations they can produce are amazing. Some of the knots are used to attach knotting materials to a support; some are used as decorative knots.

The knots shown in this section are used repeatedly throughout this book, and you'll continue to use them in all of your macramé creations. Familiarize yourself with them before you begin the projects if you haven't done macramé before. Practice the knots in a variety of random combinations, and see how they look and feel using different types of materials.

Overhand Knot

Overhand knots are unique knots in that they can be used to start or finish a piece, or they can be strictly decorative. Quite a few projects in this book utilize overhand knots; an alternating overhand knot pattern is even used to create the yoga mat bag on page 104.

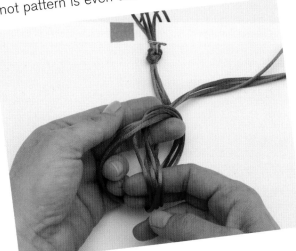

1. PULL CORDS THROUGH LOOP
Attach the material to be knotted to the top of your macramé board with T-pins to hold it securely. Hold the material loosely in one hand. With the other hand, lay the material across the tail of the cord to form a loop.

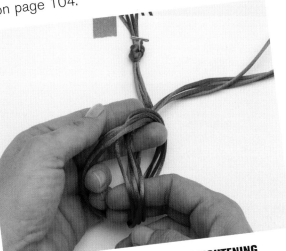

2. ADJUST KNOT PLACEMENT BEFORE TIGHTENING
Draw the tail through the loop and pull taut, but not too taut. Slide the knot to adjust its position before you tighten it completely.

3. TIGHTEN KNOT
Once the knot is in the proper placement, tighten it.

4. EXAMINE COMPLETED KNOT
Make sure the cords lay nicely before going onto the next knot.

Lark's Head Knot

The lark's head knot is primarily used as a mounting knot, attaching your material to something else, whether it is another cord or a part of a project, such as a handle, jump ring or donut bead. It's important to remember that the knot requires twice the length of materials you think you'll need, as you'll be folding it in half, creating two strands. The majority of projects in this book start by tying lark's head knots.

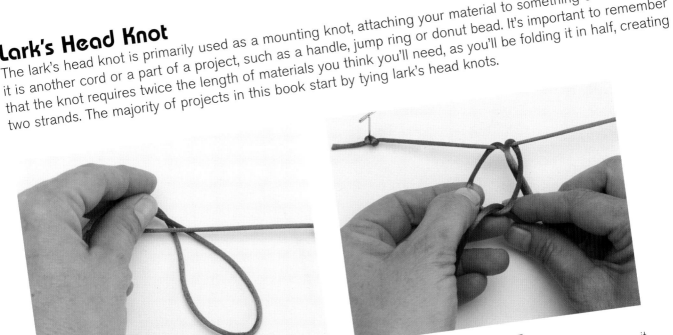

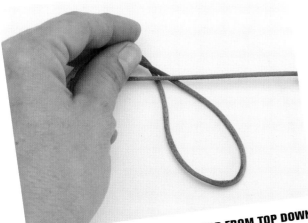

1. SLIP LOOP UNDER MOUNTING CORD FROM TOP DOWN
Anchor a small piece of cord—or whatever you want to mount your macramé to—to a dowel or jump ring. (Here, I'm using a piece of cord.) Fold the knotting materials in half and slip the loop that was formed under the mounting cord from the top down. The loop should be below the mounting cord.

2. THREAD TAILS THROUGH LOOP
Take the two tail ends of the knotting cord and pass it through the loop.

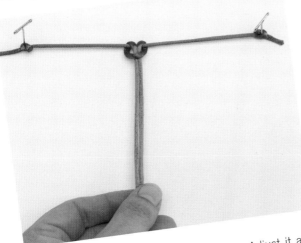

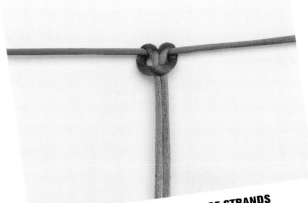

3. TIGHTEN KNOT
Pull down on the tail to tighten the knot. Adjust it as necessary.

4. CONTINUE TO DESIRED NUMBER OF STRANDS
As you can see from the finished knot, you now have 2 strands to work with. Continue mounting cords the same way until you have the desired number of strands to begin your project.

Half Knot

Half knots are among the most common macramé knots. They can be tied in two directions: to the right or to the left. Repeating half knots in the same direction forms a twist, illustrated on page 17. Pairs of alternating half knots create square knots, illustrated on page 17.

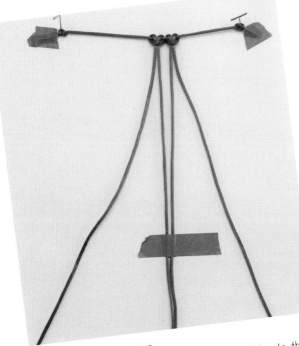

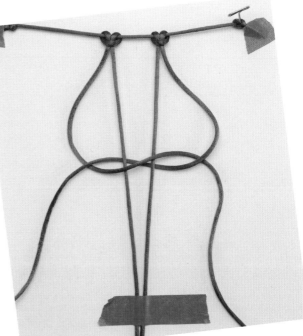

1. MOUNT FILLER CORDS

Start the half knot with at least 3 cords: 2 to do the tying and at least 1 filler cord to tie them around. (This example uses 2 fillers. The more filler cords used, the thicker the knots will be.) Throughout this book, the cords will be numbered from left to right for clarity in the instructions. Begin by anchoring the filler cords, 2 and 3, by taping them to the macramé board.

2. TIE KNOT

This half knot is being tied to the left. Cross cord 1 over 2 and 3, forming an L. Cross cord 4 over 1, and then under 2 and 3, coming up through the loop that 1 created. Cord 4 has now become cord 1 and cord 1 has become cord 4. (To tie a half knot to the right, simply reverse.)

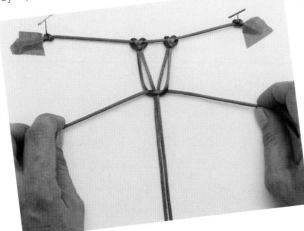

3. TIGHTEN THE KNOT

Pull 1 and 4 to tighten the knot in whatever position you'd like it to be in. Make sure your filler cords stay taut when you tighten the half knot.

tip

If your project uses knots that have filler cords, such as a square knot or repeating half knot sennit, and those filler cords will only have knots tied around them, they will require less material than the knotting cords, which are doing all of the work. The filler cords only need to be as long as the finished project plus at least 4"–6" (10cm–15cm) to allow for tying of the knot at the end. So when you measure out the materials, if you need four times the finished length amount for your knotting cords you only need just over 5 times total.

Square Knot

The square knot is one of the most popular and versatile knots. It consists of one half knot tied to the left and one half knot tied to the right.

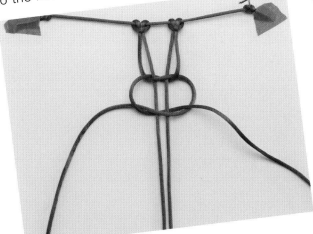

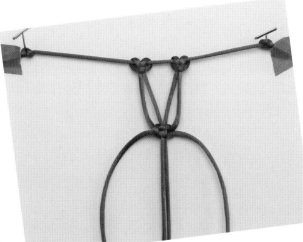

1. TIE AN ALTERNATING HALF KNOT

After tightening your first half knot, you will repeat what you did the on the other side. Cross cord 4 over 2 and 3. Cord 1 lays over 4 and then passes under 2 and 3 to come up through the loop 4 created.

2. TIGHTEN AND ADJUST

Pull 1 and 4 tight keeping 2 and 3 also taut. Adjust as necessary.

Repeating Half Knot Sennit (also Twisting or Spiral Knots)

Any continuous sequence of knots is referred to as sennit. When you repeat the tying of half knots in the same direction, always starting with the same side, the resulting knots naturally twist. This simple chain of knots is great for jewelry and straps for purses. It adds a nice textural element to macramé projects of any kind.

1. TIE SERIES OF HALF KNOTS IN ONE DIRECTION

Tie a series a half knots in the same direction (shown here: to the left). You'll start to feel your material wanting to twist. Occasionally you'll need to untape your filler cords and straighten out all of your cords by allowing the twist to occur. A good solid twist will form after about 8 half knots.

Square Knot Sennit

This sennit, or continuous sequence of knots, is simply a repeating series of square knots. Simple straps or other knotted chains that do not twist are often square knot sennits.

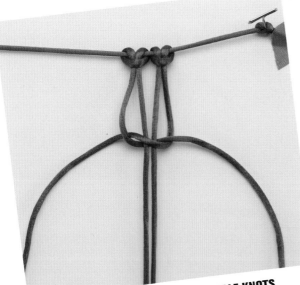

1. ALTERNATE TYING LEFT AND RIGHT HALF KNOTS
Once the first square knot is tied, tighten it and continue tying square knots until you've reached your desired length.

2. CONTINUE TO DESIRED LENGTH
This is a square knot sennit made with 3 complete square knots and one half knot. Note that on the left side of the sennit there are 3 loops, and on the right side there are 4 loops. Since these knots were started on the left side, I can count from the left to keep track of my knot count in following a pattern. The loops also show you which cord to start with next so you don't lose your place. In this example, by looking at the sennit and seeing 4 loops on the right side, I know I must start the next half-knot on the right side. This will complete the fourth square knot and, once completed, the left side will also have four loops.

Square Knot with Alternating Fillers

This knotting sequence is perfect for incorporating beads into your macramé project. The filler cord is switched back and forth and the pattern that results allows for beads to fit in the gaps. It's a simple but very effective sequence that's great for all types of jewelry, belts and straps.

1. ALTERNATE FILLER CORD FOR EACH SQUARE KNOT
Start with 4 cords. Secure cord 2 with tape and use cords 1 and 3 to tie a square knot. Switch the tape to cord 3 and tie another square knot using cords 2 and 4. Switch the tape back to cord 2 and tie another square knot using cords 1 and 3. Keep alternating until you reach your desired length. Note the gaps that form with cords 1 and 4, creating perfect spots to add beads. The button bracelet project on page 30 is based on this knot sequence.

Alternating Square Knot

The alternating square knot is widely used to fill areas with a decorative pattern. As a knot pattern, it offers a lot of design possibilities. If tied tightly, it can make an almost knit-like fabric that is often mistaken for knitting or crochet. If tied loosely, it has more of a net-like quality to it and can look rather lacey. And when building a pattern, it can be created with single square knots or doubles or some singles and some doubles.

1. BEGIN FIRST ROW
Cut 4 lengths of cord about 4' (123cm) long. Tie these on to a mounting cord using lark's head knots. You'll now have 8 cords to work with. Number them 1–8. Secure 2 and 3 to the macramé board with tape and tie a square knot with 1 and 4. Remove the tape from 2 and 3, use it to secure 6 and 7, and tie a square knot with 5 and 8.

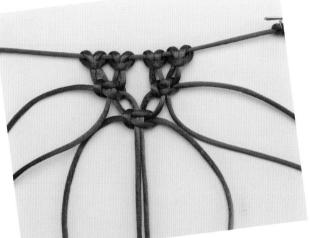

2. TIE ALTERNATING SECOND ROW
Making sure that all the knots are tight and adjust them as necessary. Start the next row by securing cords 4 and 5 and using cords 3 and 6 to tie another square knot. Notice the pattern is already starting to take shape.

3. CONTINUE TO DESIRED LENGTH
To start the next row, repeat step 1. Tighten and adjust as necessary. Now you can really start to see a pattern form. Notice the flower that has formed in the middle of the knot sequence. Continue to desired length.

Half Hitch Knot

The half hitch knot is the first half of the ever-popular double half hitch knot, seen below. On its own, the half hitch is used most often vertically where the double half hitch tends to be used horizontally or diagonally. If a half hitch knot is tied repeatedly, the resulting sennit will naturally want to twist, just like the repeated half knot. The half hitch is also used a lot in a type of macramé referred to as Cavandoli where the knot is used both vertically and horizontally to create patterns with colors. It's also referred to as Picture Macramé or Knotted Tapestry.

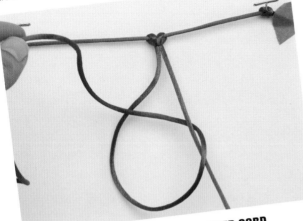

1. WRAP KNOTTING CORD AROUND FILLER CORD
Tie a length of cord with a lark's head knot onto a mounting cord, folding the cord so that one side is a third of the length and the other is two-thirds. I'm using 3' (91cm) to start, folded into two strands measuring 1' (30cm) and 2' (61cm), respectively. The longer strand is the knotting cord; the other is the filler. Bring the knotting cord over the filler and then under it, looping through and pulling tight.

2. REPEAT TO DESIRED LENGTH
Keep repeating the knot sequence of looping over, under and through until you reach a sennit long enough to naturally twist. This sennit has been knotted 7 times.

Double Half Hitch Knot

Double half hitch knots—comprised of at least four cords—are used in repeating sennits to form a perfect visual dividing line as a design element or, alternatively, a means of connecting different segments of a project to form a single unit. The knots are tied around a filler cord that directs their position, forming elements like diagonal lines, diamond shapes or even squiggles.

1. LAY KNOT BEARER OVER WORKING CORDS
Mount at least 4–5 cords with lark's head knots to a mounting cord, creating 8–10 working cords. Place a T-pin just under the first lark's head knot after cord 1. Lay cord 1 across all the other cords. This is the knot bearer, or filler cord. The other cords will then each knot around it. The T-pin helps direct the knots.

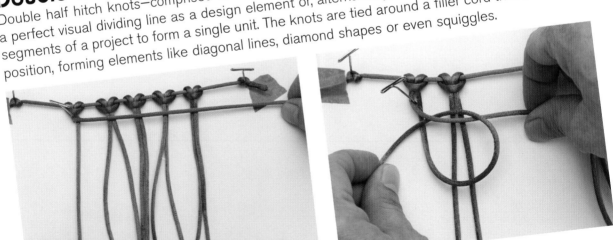

2. BEGIN TYING A HALF HITCH KNOT
Wrap cord 2 around the filler with a half hitch knot that goes over the filler cord then under and through the loop that was created.

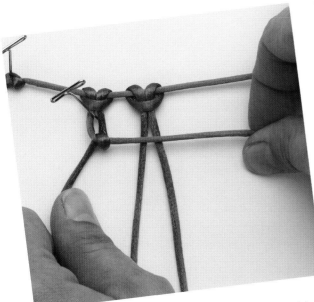

3. PULL EVERYTHING TAUT
Pull the first knot tight while keeping the filler cord held taut to ensure for a well-positioned design element.

4. COMPLETE DOUBLE HALF HITCH BY REPEATING KNOT
Repeat another half hitch knot around the filler cord using the same cord.

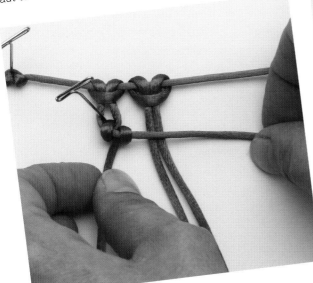

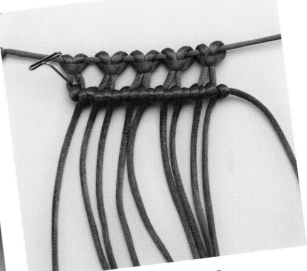

5. TIGHTEN DOUBLE HALF HITCH
The second knot reinforces the sequence and holds it in place nicely. Make sure everything is nice and tight and adjust as necessary.

6. CONTINUE ACROSS ROW OF CORDS
Keep knotting double half hitches with each cord from left to right until you've finished the row. Notice the coil that has formed.

tip
Something important to consider when you're planning a design is the amount of extra material you may need for the filler cords that will be used in double half hitch knot sequences. If you're not careful, it's easy to run out of material and you'll have to splice extra cord in, potentially compromising the design. There will be more discussion on calculating the amount of materials needed for a project on page 23.

Josephine Knot

This is my personal favorite of all the knots used in macramé. It's a pretty, decorative knot (more for aesthetics than utility). Executing this knot is a bit more complicated than the others mentioned here, but the end result is worth the effort.

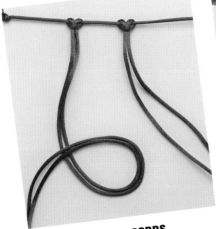

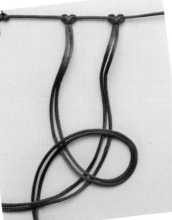

3. WRAP CORDS OVER AND UNDER
Now pass cords 3 and 4 under 1 and 2 above the loop they formed.

1. LOOP FIRST TWO CORDS
The Josephine knot is best created with more than 2 cords. This example uses 4 cords, 2 sets mounted with lark's head knots. With cords 1 and 2 create a loop that places the cords over themselves and has the loop positioned to face the center of the board. The tail ends of the cords are facing downward toward the bottom of the macramé board.

2. PASS REMAINING CORDS UNDER LOOP
Pass both cords 3 and 4 under the loop made by cords 1 and 2 and over their tail ends.

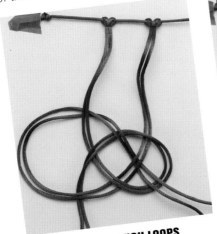

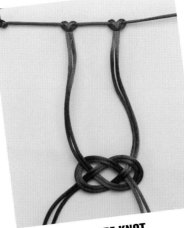

4. PASS TAIL THROUGH LOOPS
Pass cords 3 and 4 over the top of the cords 1 and 2 loop, then under themselves in the middle of the loop, and out through the loop.

5. BEGIN TO SHAPE KNOT
Carefully tighten the knot, adjusting the placement and structure of the cords.

6. COMPLETE KNOT
The tightened, complete Josephine knot should take shape as shown.

Square Knot Pattern with Alternating Knotters and Fillers

This variation of the square knot works well in sequence for creating purse straps and belts. By switching the fillers and the knotters with each alternating knot, you can balance out your material usage. You can also use it in sequence to introduce color play into your macramé. Simply select knotters and fillers of different colors, and tie your knots tightly to hide the fillers. When you switch the placement of the cord pairs, you'll also switch colors.

1. TIE SQUARE KNOT AND SWITCH CORDS
Mount 2 cords on your mounting cord to yield 4 cords. Secure cords 2 and 3 with tape and tie a square knot with 1 and 4. Remove the tape and secure 1 and 4 with tape.

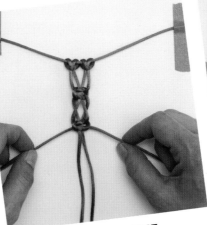

2. TIE SECOND SQUARE KNOT
Tie another square knot this time using cords 2 and 3 Tighten and adjust your knot, making sure your cords are nice and taut.

3. ALTERNATE CORDS AND REPEAT
Again switch cords 2 and 3 with 1 and 4 and tie another square knot. Notice the pattern that forms in the sequence.

Calculating the Amount of Material You'll Need

Macramé requires that you mount all of your materials before you start tying your knots. This is where it differs greatly from knitting or crocheting. With those crafts, you use the yarn as you go, working from a skein. With macramé, you need to determine the required amount of material first, and then mount it. Managing your material becomes very important. In most cases, you'll need yards or meters of material for even small projects. It can be a little intimidating at first, but with a little practice, you can estimate your needs accurately before beginning any project.

The more complicated the knots your pattern calls for, the more material you'll need. If your design has a lot of areas with half or double half hitch knots, you'll need to compensate for that, since those knots use up a lot of cord. The projects in this book give you material quantities, but if you want to experiment with variations or with your own macramé designs, you'll need to have a basic understanding of how to determine the amount of material you will require.

Most often, you'll need each cord to be at least four to six times what the finished length of your project will be. This is a lot of cord or yarn, which can be a bit of a hassle to deal with. The extra long ends are carefully gathered up with various forms of bobbins to make managing the yardage easier. Two types of bobbins are featured on page 24.

Occasionally, you can save materials if you are knotting sequences that don't change the filler cords, like with a simple belt made from square knots and/or twist knots. When those cords are mounted, the fillers should be just longer than your finished length. The knotting cords will then be about 4 times the final length. A little extra material should be given to tie off at the end. It is always good to have extra rather than not enough. If you find yourself with extra materials after you complete your project, you may want to reference that in a notebook. Then, if you want to re-create a project later, you can purchase a more accurate amount.

Using Bobbins for Thin Cords

When a project requires long lengths of cords, bobbins can make them easier to manage and prevent them from becoming a tangled mess. Any bobbins will work, but the plastic bobbins shown here are some of the best I've found for working with thin cord. (If you're using a thick material, like yarn, see the method below, instead.) Bobbins allow you to wrap the material on a spool, then encapsulate the wrapped length inside. These bobbins are available at local bead or craft retailers or online.

1. WIND CORD AROUND BOBBIN
Wrap the extra cord around the core of the bobbin as if loading a yo-yo.

2. SEAL WOUND CORD INSIDE
Once you've wrapped up enough material, close the bobbin to trap the cord and keep it from unrolling.

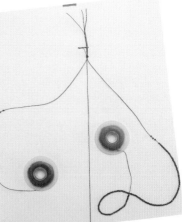

3. UNWIND MATERIAL AS NEEDED
With the cords tied into their bobbins, they're a lot easier to work with. These bobbins allow you to unwind your material as you need it.

Bundling Thicker Fibers

As much as I love the plastic bobbins, when you're working with thick materials, like yarn or leather lace, you'll need some other way to manage your materials. This is my favorite method.

1. WIND AND TIE MATERIALS
Wind the length of yarn or other thick material around your hand. Secure it with a piece of cord in a contrasting color. When you need more material, simply untie, unwrap, then retie.

Securing a Knot with Glue

Most macramé projects end with the same step: glue and trim. Securing the final knot(s) of your project with a bit of adhesive before you trim the excess length of cords ensures that your hard work won't unravel with wear and tear.

1. GLUE AND TRIM
With a T-pin, apply a small amount of white glue to the inside of the project's final knot(s) and around it at its start and finish. Tighten the knot and wipe away any excess glue. Allow the glue to dry completely before trimming the end of the cord as close to the knot as possible.

JEWELRY TECHNIQUES

While macramé is at the core of all this book's projects, the jewelry projects require a few other basic jewelry-making techniques to complete them. If you're a beginner, don't despair: They're all outlined for you step by step here. You'll need to have round-nose pliers, chain-nose pliers and wire cutters handy (see Tools on page 12).

Wire Wrapping

Wire wrapping is a secure and durable way to create links to add chain, charms, beads or findings. If you're a beginner, choose an inexpensive, thinner-gauge wire to start (thicker gauges can be difficult to manipulate).

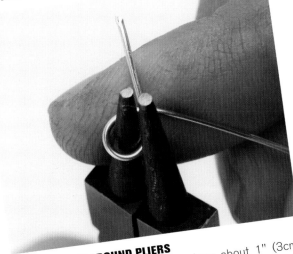

1. WRAP LOOP AROUND PLIERS
Use round-nose pliers to wrap a loop about 1" (3cm) from the end of your length of wire. Use your finger to help guide the tail into place. The tail should be at a 90-degree angle to the body of the wire and the loop that was formed. If you want to attach a piece of chain, jump ring or another link, thread it onto the loop now before wrapping it closed.

2. HOLD LOOP AND WRAP TAIL
Remove the pliers from the inside of the loop and use them to grasp the loop instead. Using chain nose pliers, grasp the tail of the wire and wrap it around the body of the wire, just below the loop.

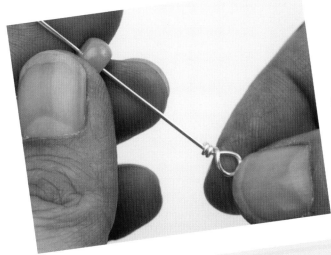

3. FINISH WRAP AND TRIM
Wrap the tail around the wire 2 or 3 times. Trim any excess with wire cutters. Use chain-nose pliers to squeeze the wraps, making sure the end of the wire isn't poking out so it won't scratch the wearer. Add your bead, chain or finding and wrap another loop flush against it, as in step 1. Again thread on any chain, jump rings or other links desired before wrapping the link closed, as in step 2.

Making Ear Wires

Store-bought ear wires for earrings are available in a variety of shapes, sizes, styles and types of metal. If you're like me and you prefer to make everything yourself if possible, you can follow these simple steps to make your own. The only additional tools you'll need are a dowel and maybe a metal file or emery board.

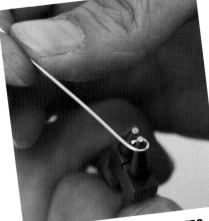

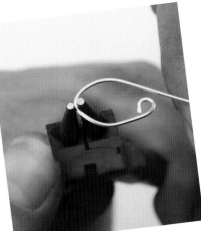

1. WRAP SMALL LOOP WITH PLIERS
Cut 2 lengths of wire to 2" (5cm) each. Using the round-nose pliers, grasp the end of one wire and make a small loop. Repeat with the other wire.

2. USE DOWEL TO SHAPE
Hold the wire at the loop and gently wrap it around the dowel to shape it. Again, repeat this step with the other piece of wire to ensure the pair of ear wires match.

3. SLIGHTLY BEND EAR WIRES
With round-nose pliers, make a small bend at the top of the ear wire to help it sit in the ear. Remove any sharp edges from the wires with a file or emery board.

Making a Decorative Clasp

Again, you can buy a variety of decorative clasps for your jewelry projects, or you can follow these simple steps to make your own. I designed these years ago and favor them over anything I've seen in a store. These clasps can be made any size you like and from a variety of wire gauges and metal types.

1. HAMMER THE END OF THE WIRE FLAT
Start with a piece of sterling silver 16–18g wire about 2½" (6cm) long. Set it on a bench block and use a jewelry hammer to pound one of the ends of the wire flat.

2. WRAP THE END WITH ROUND-NOSE PLIERS
Use the round-nose pliers to wrap a small decorative loop at the end of the wire. This small loop is also functional since it gives the hook a smooth end to pass through the other side's loop to connect the necklace.

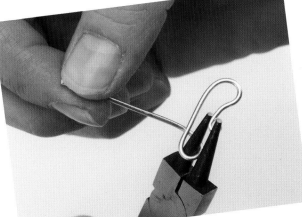

3. FORM BODY OF CLASP AROUND PLIERS
Still using the round-nose pliers, grip the wire about ¼" (6mm) down from the first small loop and wrap the wire around the thick part of the pliers in the opposite direction of the first loop. Now you have a hook. Adjust the hook as needed with your fingers and the pliers.

4. WRAP LOOP END HOOK OF CLASP
The loop that connects the hook to the rest of the neck-lace now needs to be formed. Using the round-nose pliers, start a wire wrap loop about ⅛" (3mm) below the bottom of the hook.

5. CLOSE LOOP BY WRAPPING WHILE HOLDING LOOP
Grasp the loop just made with the pliers and wrap the tail of the wire around 2–3 times to form a nice coil.

6. TRIM END CLOSE TO WRAP
Trim any excess wire and smooth the end with a file if it's sharp.

7. HAMMER TO WORK-HARDEN CLASP
Once the shape of the hook is com-pleted and you're satisfied, hammer the body of the hook lightly on the bench block. This will flatten the hook and, more important, work-harden the metal. "Work-hardening" is a process that strengthens the metal, making it stiffer and less likely to lose its shape.

PART 1: JEWELRY

My first real exposure to macramé was at a store called Macraménia, which sold beads of all kinds and other jewelry-making supplies, as well as materials to macramé with. But it was the storeowner's jewelry that left the greatest impression on me. Most of her pieces were created with complex knot sequences in combination with amazing centerpieces and beads. She worked with semiprecious gemstones and beads and what seemed to be the most exotic materials. The pieces were art, one-of-a-kind art to wear.

I'm a simple designer, though, with a deep appreciaton for fine design and excellent craftsmanship in any piece of jewelry. I like to explore different jewelry-making techniques and have learned quite a few, but I always seem to come back to macramé. It's a craft with admirable simplicity, requiring minimal tools and materials. Most of the designs on the following pages reflect that—and a few of them were even inspired by my experiences at Macraménia back in the 1970s.

This chapter is filled with a selection of jewelry projects that use macramé in ways you may never have expected. We'll explore wire wrapping in versatile ways, showcasing beads in the Wire-Wrapped Necklace and Earrings (page 50), letting the wire take center stage in the Turquoise Donut and Wire Bracelet (page 56) and combining the two in the surprisingly delicate Pearl Chandelier Earrings (page 60). We'll move beyond traditional knotting and jewelry techniques when we dabble in mold-making and metal clay (and even get to play with fire!) in the Metal Clay Josephine Bracelet (page 74). We'll string dainty seed beads to create beaded macramé cord in the Red Seed Bead Spiral Necklace (page 34) and the Bead Framing Bead Bracelet (page 38). And who doesn't like to indulge in a little leather occasionally? The Leather Power Cuff Bracelet (page 64) is a great project that brings together leather and wire for a big impact.

Projects increase in difficulty throughout the chapter, so choose accordingly—but the step-by-step instructions and photos make them all accessible to even beginning crafters. Once you see how fun the techniques are and what a joy the materials are to work with, you'll want to macramé more and more. Pretty soon you might even be designing your own mod knots!

BUTTON AND BEADS BRACELET

The square knot with alternating fillers (see page 18) used to construct this bracelet is just fabulous. Switching back and forth between filler cords makes a perfect knot sequence for beads: The beads become the focus and the knots just melt back into the scenery. Of course, the button clasp makes a nice design statement, too.

Mod Knots

overhand knot
(see page 14)

square knot with
alternating fillers
(see page 18)

Mod Materials

4 2' (61cm) lengths
of 4-ply khaki waxed linen

1 fancy button for
the clasp

62 extra-small rondelles

21 oval, faceted
amazonite beads

macramé board

T-pins

masking tape

craft glue

scissors

plastic bobbins

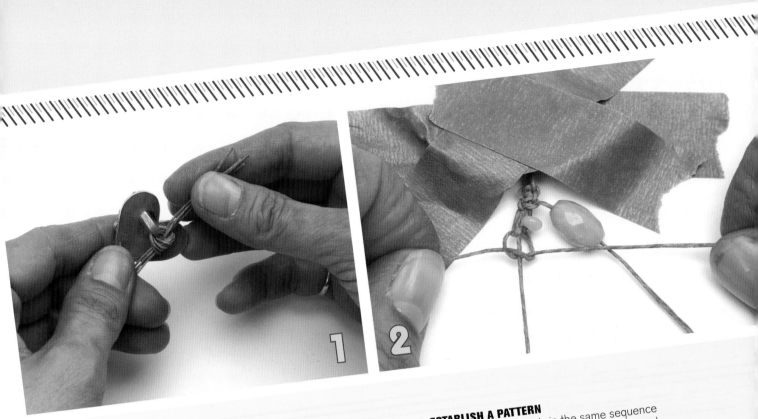

1. TIE THE CORDS TO THE BUTTON
Use an overhand knot to tie the 4 strands of waxed linen to the back of the button. Glue the knot and let it dry completely. Trim the excess as close to the knot as possible.

2. TAPE BUTTON TO SECURE AND BEGIN KNOTTING
Tape down the button securely. Tie 2 square knots. Thread an oval bead onto cord 4 and thread a rondelle onto cord 3. Tape cord 2 down to keep it tight and tie a square knot with cords 1 and 3.

3. ADD BEADS WHILE KNOTTING
Remove the tape holding cord 2 down. Thread an oval bead onto cord 1 and thread 2 rondelles onto cord 2. Tape down cord 3 and tie a square knot with cords 2 and 4. Thread a rondelle onto cord 3.

4. ESTABLISH A PATTERN
Continue threading beads in the same sequence as well as continue switching cords back and forth. Notice the pattern that's forming.

5: COMPLETE CLASP LOOP
Once the desired length for the bracelet is reached, begin stringing the rondelles onto cord 1. This piece will become the loop that passes over the button to close the bracelet. Periodically test the length of the loop by comparing it to the button, and continue stringing until the appropriate length is reached. Tie the loop to the bracelet with strand 4 in an overhand knot. Glue the knot and allow it to dry before cutting the ends close.

SQUARE KNOT CHARM NECKLACE

Here the versatility of the square knot is highlighted by charms added to a simple sennit of square knots. But its simplicity is deceptive. This necklace requires long strands of waxed linen, which will need to be managed properly, or you can end up with a tangled mess of cords. But the results of this necklace are worth the wrangling.

Mod Knots

overhand knot (see page 14)

lark's head knot
(see page 15)

square knot sennit
(see page 18)

Mod Materials

4 24' (732cm) strands of 2-ply marine blue waxed linen

1 large Bali silver swirl charm

8 small Bali silver swirl charms

6 small blue glass beads

6 decorative sterling silver headpins

2 decorative fancy hook clasps

1 large jump ring

plastic bobbins

macramé board

T-pins

masking tape

craft glue

scissors

round-nose pliers

chain-nose pliers

wire cutters

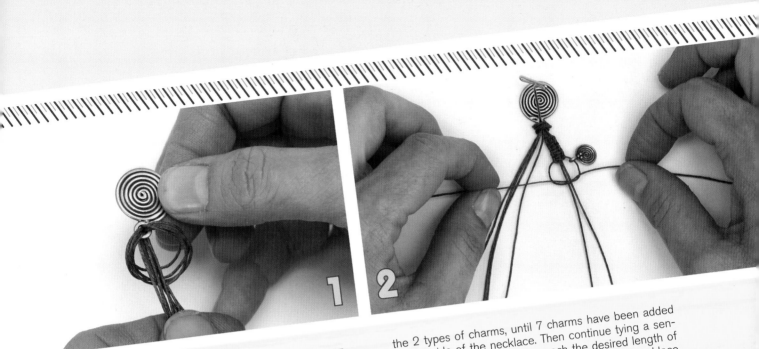

1. PREPARE CHARMS AND KNOT LINEN CORDS TO CENTERPIECE

Create 6 charms by threading a small blue glass bead onto each decorative headpin and using your chain-nose pliers to wire wrap (see page 25) a loop just above each bead to make it into a charm. Set them aside. Hold your 4 lengths of 24' (732cm) waxed linen flush together, fold them in half and mount onto the large Bali silver swirl charm with a lark's head knot. Be careful not to tangle your linen.

2. SECURE CHARM ON BOARD AND BEGIN KNOTTING

Pin this piece to your macramé board with the cords facing you. Wind the ends of the cords in encapsulating plastic bobbins (see page 24). Separate the 8 strands into 2 sets of 4 strands—a set for each side of the necklace—and tape down the 2 center strands of each. Begin with the first set of strands and tie 4 complete square knots. Thread a small spiral charm onto cord 4 and tie another square knot.

3. TIE SQUARE KNOT SENNIT AND ADD CHARM

Tie a sennit of 9 square knots. Thread 1 of the charms you created in step 1 onto cord 4. Tie another sennit of 9 square knots.

4. ESTABLISH PATTERN OF SENNITS AND ALTERNATING CHARMS

When the sennit is complete, add a small Bali silver swirl charm to cord 4. Continue repeating the pattern of tying sennits of 9 square knots and adding 1 charm to cord 4, alternating between

the 2 types of charms, until 7 charms have been added to that side of the necklace. Then continue tying a sennit of square knots until you reach the desired length of your necklace. Repeat for the other side of the necklace (again starting with a sennit of 4 square knots and small spiral charm for symmetry). Add your charms for this side of the necklace onto cord 1. When the 2 sides are even lengths, tie a hook clasp onto each end with an overhand knot. Coat each knot with a dot of craft glue, let it dry and then trim the ends.

> ### tip
>
> Having hook clasps on both ends of the necklace makes it easy to add extenders, such as a jump ring or piece of chain, or even to add another necklace so you can wear two strands at once. (I think this would be fabulous paired with the red seed bead necklace on page 34.)

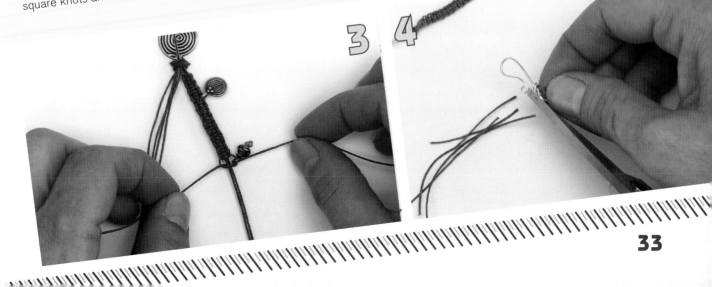

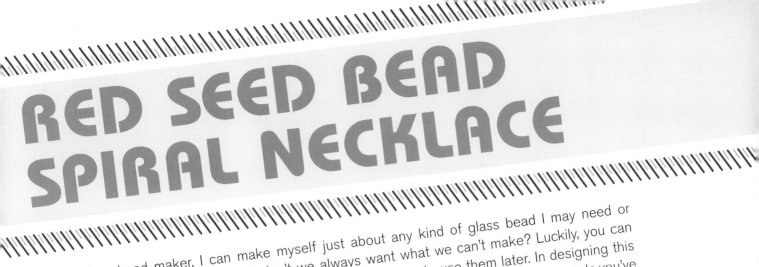

RED SEED BEAD SPIRAL NECKLACE

As a glass bead maker, I can make myself just about any kind of glass bead I may need or want—except for seed beads. And don't we always want what we can't make? Luckily, you can find seed beads everywhere. So I buy them, always planning to use them later. In designing this necklace, I decided later is now! (Does that make sense? Sure it does.) Go get seed beads you've been squirreling away and make this necklace. It takes the beloved repeated half knot and adds a little sparkle and color to the mix. Each knot has a seed bead on each side. What a pretty necklace this is. And the pattern translates really well for use with other larger beads; just make sure the knotting material is strong enough to handle them.

Mod Knots

overhand knot
(see page 14)

repeating half knot sennit
(see page 17)

Mod Materials

2 8' (244cm) lengths of
crimson 2-ply waxed linen

1 2' (61cm) length of
crimson 2-ply waxed linen

approximately 500 seed
beads in one color

2 hook clasps (see page 26)

plastic bobbins

macramé board

T-pins

masking tape

craft glue

scissors

1. THREAD SEED BEADS ONTO WAXED LINEN
Begin threading seed beads onto one of the 8' (244cm) strands of waxed linen.

2. COMPLETE FIRST CORD AND FINISH SECOND STRAND
Continue stringing until the length of beaded waxed linen reaches about 2' (61cm) in beaded length, leaving the end on a 6' (183cm) coil. (This is more than is needed, but it's easier to deal with all of the beads now rather than later.) Repeat for a second strand.

3. TIE OVERHAND KNOT AND SECURE STRANDS TO BOARD
Tie the 2 beaded strands and 2' (61cm) strand of waxed linent together in an overhand knot (this knot will be removed later and replaced with a clasp), leaving about 4" (10cm) of extra length at the top to work with at a later

time. Allow the beads to naturally slide down to the coil so they're out of your way, as shown. Use a T-pin to pin the knot to a macramé board. The unbeaded strand will be the filler cord; secure it to the board with masking tape. Wind the bottom of each strand around a plastic bobbin to make the strands more manageable to work with. Here I am using plastic bobbins that collapse to hold your working strand in place, as illustrated on page 24.

4. TIE HALF KNOT AND ADD FIRST TWO BEADS
Tie a half knot to the left. Slide one bead all the way up each of the left and right strands. Tie another half knot in the same direction and make sure the beads are correctly secured in position.

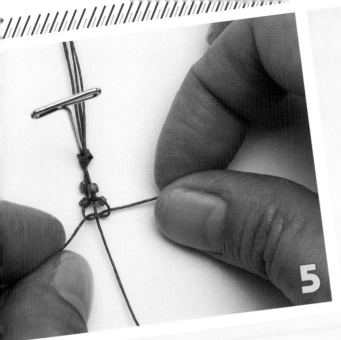

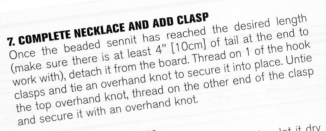

5. CONTINUE ALTERNATING BEADS AND KNOTS

Slide one more bead up each outer strand. Tie a half knot and again tighten everything into place. Here you can see how the beads are secured into alignment by the knots along the filler strand.

6. KNOT TWISTED, BEADED SENNIT

Continue in this way for the length of the entire strand. You'll notice the strand begin to twist as you work. Let it twist, occasionally sliding the knotting strands under the filler and trading sides to allow the twist to naturally form.

7. COMPLETE NECKLACE AND ADD CLASP

Once the beaded sennit has reached the desired length (make sure there is at least 4" [10cm] of tail at the end to work with), detach it from the board. Thread on 1 of the hook clasps and tie an overhand knot to secure it into place. Untie the top overhand knot, thread on the other end of the clasp and secure it with an overhand knot.

8. SECURE KNOT AND TRIM

Secure each of the knots with a dot of craft glue, let it dry and then trim the ends flush with the necklace (securing the knots allows you to cut the ends close).

BEAD FRAMING
BEAD BRACELET

Here it is, all glass, all the time. I love tiny beads and am always trying to figure out interesting ways to incorporate them into macramé. They can be a bit of a struggle to manage, however. This bracelet uses strands of seed beads as the knotting material, and when they're tied, they surround the lampwork bead strung on the filler, and frame those beads beautifully. The stringing wire is plastic coated steel that is attached to the clasp with crimp beads.

Mod Knots

square knot (see page 17)

Mod Materials

Soft Flex "Soft Touch" beading wire .019 cut to 3 lengths: 12" (30cm) for the center strand, and 2 lengths of 2' (61cm) for the outer strands

9 silver crimp beads

1 hank of amber seed beads

7 handmade lampwork glass beads, with holes big enough to pass a strand of seed beads through

sterling silver triple strand clasp

macramé board

T-pins

crimping pliers

wire cutters

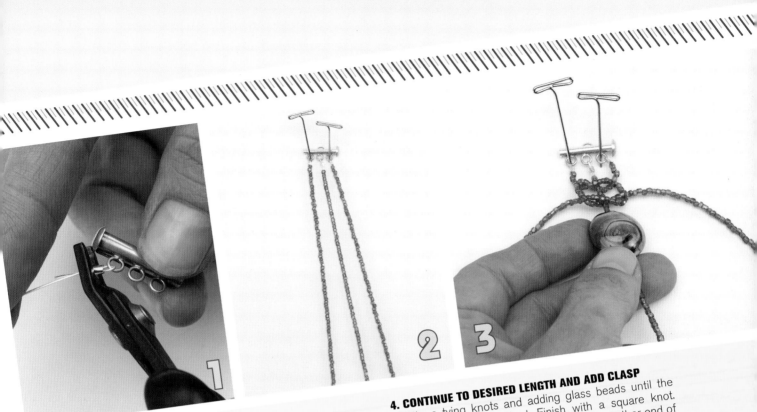

1. CRIMP WIRE STRANDS TO CLASP

Thread one of the longer pieces of wire with a crimp bead. Pass the wire through one of the loops on the clasp and back through the crimp bead. Pull the crimp bead as close to the loop as possible and use the crimping pliers to secure it in place. Trim the excess wire as close as possible. Attach a strand of wire to each of the other loops in the same way, with the shortest strand in the center.

2. STRING SEED BEADS ONTO WIRE

String the seed beads onto the three strands of beading wire. Make sure the beads are strung on tightly, leaving no space or gaps between them. Add a crimp bead to the end of each strand to hold the beads on, making sure it's tight so the beads don't fall off or loosen while the strands are being knotted.

3. TIE KNOT AND ADD GLASS BEAD

Tie a square knot and then thread a lampwork glass bead onto the filler strand.

4. CONTINUE TO DESIRED LENGTH AND ADD CLASP

Continue tying knots and adding glass beads until the desired length is reached. Finish with a square knot. Carefully crimp each of the wire ends to the other end of the clasp, as in step 1. Remove excess beads as needed before crimping each wire to the loop. There may be varying amounts of extra beads and wire on each cord, so each one should be handled one at a time, carefully.

5. TRIM EXCESS

Trim the excess beading wire as close to the crimp bead as possible.

tip

Soft Flex brand's "Soft Touch" beading wire has amazing flexibility as well as durability. It also doesn't kink as easily as some beading wires do.

SHIBUICHI LENTIL NECKLACE

I am blessed to know some incredibly talented bead artists. Many of them are glass bead makers and some are metalsmiths. This necklace showcases the work of a couple of these people. The focal bead is made from an alloy of copper and silver, known as shibuichi, which was first formulated in Japan. The surface color of the bead inspired my color choices for this project as well as the bead and knot combinations.

Mod Knots

overhand knot
(see page 14)

repeating half knot sennit
(see page 17)

Mod Materials

4 4' (122cm) lengths
purple 4-ply waxed linen

8 3' (91cm) lengths
purple 4-ply waxed linen

2 3' (91cm) lengths
pink 4-ply waxed linen

large Shibuichi Lentil bead
(by Lea Anne Hartman)

7 large purple borosilicate
beads (by Dan Eister)

46 extra-small dichroic
beads in purples and pinks

macramé board

T-pins

masking tape

craft glue

scissors

plastic bobbins

1. BEGIN NECKLACE AND ADD FOCAL BEAD

Gather all 14 strands of waxed linen, with their ends lined up evenly, and tie an overhand knot about 6" (15cm) from the end, and slide on the large shibuichi lentil bead, making sure the knot is holding it securely in place.

2. BEGIN HALF KNOT SENNIT

Pin the knot to your macramé board and slide the shibuichi bead snugly up against it. Divide the strands into 2 groups of 7—each with 2 long purple strands, 4 short purple strands and 1 pink strand—on your macramé board to begin the 2 sides of the necklace. Begin with one side. Arrange the strands so cords 1 and 4 are the longer purple cords, and the pink is cord 7. Wrap the long strands in plastic bobbins. Secure 2 and 3 to the board with tape and tie a sennit of repeating half knots with 1 and 4 until the resulting twist reaches about 2" (5cm) (about 45 knots, 6 full twists).

3. ADD ACCENT BEADS AS YOU WORK

On strands 5, 6 and 7, begin randomly spacing small dichroic beads onto the loose strands, securing each with an overhand knot directly above it and another one below it. Here I'm adding 2 beads to each of 2 loose strands, and 1 to the remaining strand. Keep these beads within the same vertical space as the completed portion of the twist knot.

4. ADD BEAD AND SIMPLIFY CHAIN

Thread on a large borosilicate bead over all 7 strands and slide it so it sits where the knots end; it will naturally rest on the highest small bead below it. Tape 1 of the short purple strands with the other fillers, so now there are 3. Begin tying another series of repeating half knots with 1 and 4, the longer purple cords. Notice that with the new filler, you're absorbing one of the loose strands into the twist knot. Continue the sennit for 2" (5cm).

5. REPEAT TO COMPLETE OTHER SIDE

Repeat steps 3 and 4 until you've reached the desired length and all the loose strands have been absorbed. Tie an overhand knot, thread on a borosilicate bead and secure it in place with an overhand knot. Glue the ends and trim when completely dry. Repeat steps 2–5 for the other side of the necklace. When dividing the strands for this side it's the reverse of the other side. Strand 1 will be the pink strand and the knotting cords will be 4 and 7. At the end, tie an overhand knot. Then, form the excess cord into a loop just big enough to fit over the last borosilicate bead that was tied onto the other side, and tie an overhand knot to complete the clasp. Glue the knots, let dry and trim the ends.

QUAD-STRAND TWIST NECKLACE

I think one of the luxuries of macramé is using colorful materials to knot with—especially when working a twist of repeating half knots. I really enjoy this technique when I can indulge in making something that showcases both color and form, like this quad-strand necklace.

Mod Knots

overhand knot
(see page 14)

repeating half knot sennit
(see page 17)

Mod Materials

3 6' (183cm) lengths teal 4-ply waxed linen

3 6' (183cm) lengths turquoise 4-ply waxed linen

3 9' (274cm) lengths marine blue 4-ply waxed linen

3 9' (274cm) lengths purple 4-ply waxed linen

2 large decorative bead caps or cones (I made these out of metal clay, but you can purchase an assortment at your local bead or craft store)

1 decorative clasp to coordinate with the cones

macramé board

T-pins

masking tape

craft glue

scissors

plastic bobbins

1. BEGIN FOUR SEPARATE SOLID-COLORED TWISTING SENNITS

Section your strands of waxed linen by color, hold the ends flush and, 6" (15cm) from the end of each group of cords, tie an overhand knot. Secure each set to the macramé board and wind the strands on plastic bobbins. Begin knotting each trio of strands in sennits of repeating half knots.

2. COMPLETE SENNITS AND REPOSITION STRANDS

Continue until each is the desired length of the focal area, or center, of the necklace (these are about 8" [20cm] long), staggering the lengths very slightly so they don't all end up sitting on top of each other. Remove the overhand knot you've tied at the end of each sennit and line up the unknotted ends. Flip the end of each sennit and line up the knots. The longer marine blue sennit around and line up the knots. The longer blue strands will wrap around the others to complete that side of the necklace later. Leave 2 of the purple strands on bobbins and pull them off to the sides. Trim all the other cords to a length of about 5–6" (13–15cm).

3. TIE PURPLE STRANDS AROUND OTHERS

Begin tying the purple strands around all the center strands in a sennit of repeating left half knots. Notice the thickness of the twist that forms. This will serve as one side of the necklace surrounding the focal section you created in steps 1–2. Continue until this half of the necklace has reached the desired length.

4. SLIDE ON DECORATIVE CONE

Remove the piece from your macramé board. Slide a decorative bead cap down to where all the strands connect to hide that spot.

5. FINISH OTHER SIDE AND ADD CLASP

Start on the other side of the necklace by gathering the unknotted sections, laying them together, positioning the marine blue strands off to either side, and securing all the others with tape. Trim the filler cords to a length of 5–6" (13–15cm). Repeat steps 3–4 using the blue strands to tie a repeating half knot sennit around the others until the length is even with the other side. Tie each group of strands to the clasp with an overhand knot. Glue the knots, let them dry and trim the ends.

SWALLOW NECKLACE AND EARRINGS SET

So I've become addicted to the online craft marketplace www.etsy.com, both as a seller and as a buyer. That's where I found these small swallow charms—they're all over etsy.com, showcased in really lovely pieces of jewelry. This project uses a nice variety of knots and a sprinkling of tiny seed beads to accent the little birds.

Mod Knots

Necklace

overhand knot
(see page 14)

lark's head knot
(see page 15)

repeating half knot
sennit (see page 17)

alternating square knot
(see page 19)

double half hitch knot
(see page 20)

Earrings

half hitch knot
(see page 20)

Mod Materials

Necklace

8 8' (244cm) lengths ivory 2-ply
waxed linen

large antique brass
swallow charm

4 small antique brass
swallow charms

antique brass hook clasp

an assortment of seed
beads (Aiko) in Satin Sea
Serpent Green AB, Matte
Raku Teal/Blue Iris and Matte
Raku Steel Blue

macramé board

T-pins

masking tape

craft glue

scissors

Earrings

2 2' (61cm) lengths ivory
2-ply waxed linen

2 ½" (1cm) diameter jump
rings

2 small antique brass
swallow charms

18 seed beads (Aiko) in
an assortment of Satin
Sea Serpent Green AB,
Matte Raku Teal/Blue
Iris and Matte Raku
Steel Blue

2 oversized antique
brass ear wires

craft glue

scissors

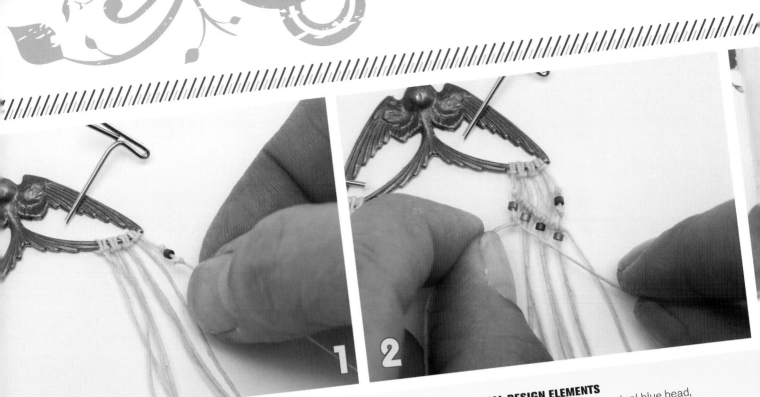

Necklace

1. BEGIN NECKLACE

One at a time, tie 4 strands of the ivory waxed linen onto each side of the swallow centerpiece with lark's head knots, which gives you 8 strands on each side. Pin the centerpiece to the macramé board. Start on the right side of the necklace, tie an overhand knot with strand 8 and thread on a teal/blue seed bead. Secure the bead in place with another overhand knot.

2. CREATE DIAGONAL SERIES OF DOUBLE HALF HITCH KNOTS

Lay strand 1 at a slight diagonal across strands 2–8. This will be the knot bearer for a line of double half hitch knots. One at a time, knot each of the 7 strands to strand 1 using a double half hitch. Strand 1 now becomes strand 8. Thread 1 seed bead onto each of strands 1, 3, 5 and 7 in this color order: green, steel blue, teal/blue, green. Lay strand 1 at a slight diagonal across strands 2–8. Again knot each of the 7 strands to strand 1 using a double half hitch. Strand 1 now becomes strand 8.

3. CONTINUE DIAGONAL DESIGN ELEMENTS

Tie an overhand knot on strand 1, thread on a steel blue bead, and secure it with an overhand knot. Lay 8 across strands 1–7 at a diagonal and one at a time, starting with strand 7, knot each of the strands to the knot bearer with a double half hitch. Strand 8 is now 1. Begin the first row of the alternating square knot pattern: Tie a square knot with strands 1 and 4 around fillers 2 and 3. String a teal/blue seed bead onto 1 and a steel blue seed bead onto 4. Tie a square knot with 5 and 8 around fillers 6 and 7. String a green seed bead onto 5 and a steel blue seed bead onto 8.

4. CONTINUE KNOTTING AND ADD SWALLOW CHARM

Continue with 2 more rows of alternating square knots, without adding any seed beads in these rows. With strand 8, leave a little bit of space, tie an overhand knot, slide on the small swallow charm and tie another overhand knot. Make sure to use a swallow that will be flying toward the inside of the necklace.

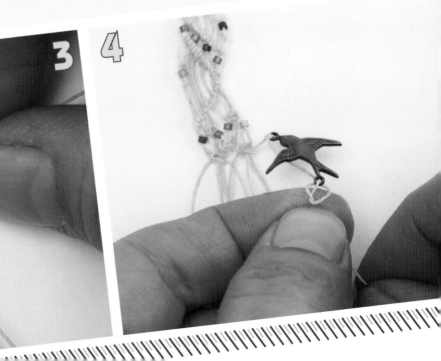

5

6

5. THREAD ON SEED BEADS AND TIE OVERHAND KNOTS
Among strands 1–7, randomly secure seed beads in assorted colors with pairs of overhand knots for a vertical space of about ½" (1cm). Then, tie together pairs of strands—1 and 2, 3 and 4, 5 and 6, and 7 and 8—each with an overhand knot forming a diagonal line, as shown.

6. ESTABLISH PATTERN OF SQUARE KNOTS AND SEED BEADS
Take strands 1 and 2 in one hand and 7 and 8 in the other and tie them in a double-thickness square knot around 3–6. Thread 3 assorted seed beads onto strand 1 and 3 seed beads onto strand 8. Repeat the double-thickness square knot. Thread 3 assorted seed beads onto strand 1 and 3 seed beads onto strand 8. Repeat the double-thickness square knot. Again thread 3 assorted seed beads onto strand 1 and 3 seed beads onto strand 8. Repeat the double-thickness square knot.

7. ADD SWALLOW CHARM AND TIE DOUBLE HALF HITCH KNOT
Thread the swallow charm onto strands 1 (the tail end) and 8 (the nose end), sliding it down to rest on top of strands 2–7, securing it with an overhand knot on each strand. This time the swallow should face the opposite direction from the first swallow. Thread 5 seed beads onto strand 1, lay it diagonally over the other strands, and tie them each, one at a time, to this strand with a double half hitch knot. Strand 1 now becomes strand 8.

7

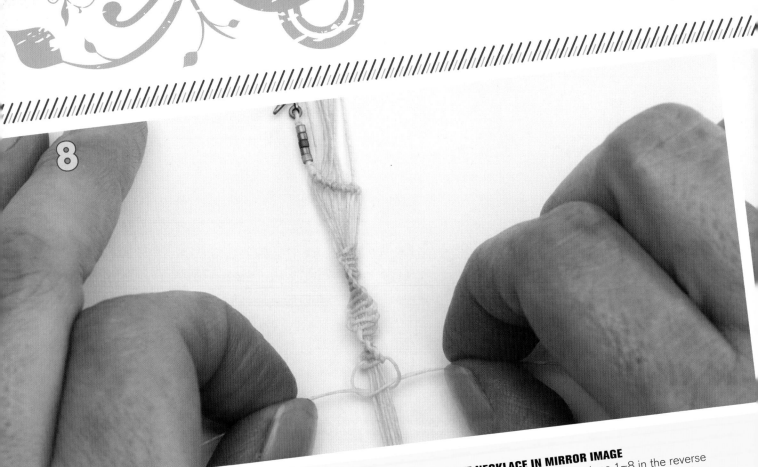

8. TIE TWISTING SENNIT OF REPEATING HALF KNOTS
Leave about ½" (1cm) of vertical space and then begin tying a sennit of repeating half knots in a twist, using strands 1 and 8 to tie around fillers 2–7. Continue the nice, thick twist for about 1" (3cm).

9. TIE EVENLY SPACED SQUARE KNOTS
Tie four square knots with strands 1 and 8 around fillers 2–7 in ½" (1cm) increments.

10. COMPLETE NECKLACE IN MIRROR IMAGE
Repeat on the other side, executing steps 1–8 in the reverse direction to create the mirror image of one side on the other side. Finish by tying one half of the clasp to each end of the necklace with an overhand knot. Coat these knots with craft glue, let them dry completely and trim the ends.

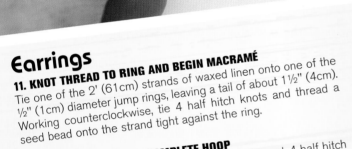

Earrings

11. KNOT THREAD TO RING AND BEGIN MACRAMÉ

Tie one of the 2' (61cm) strands of waxed linen onto one of the ½" (1cm) diameter jump rings, leaving a tail of about 1½" (4cm). Working counterclockwise, tie 4 half hitch knots and thread a seed bead onto the strand tight against the ring.

12. REPEAT PATTERN TO COMPLETE HOOP

Repeat in this pattern: 4 half hitch knots, seed bead, 4 half hitch knots, nose end of swallow charm, 4 half hitch knots, seed bead, 4 half hitch knots, tail end of swallow charm, 4 half hitch knots, seed bead, 4 half hitch knots with seed beads until the entire hoop is covered. Use the working strand and the tail of the first knot to tie the ear wire onto the earring. Coat the knot with glue, let it dry and trim the ends close.

tip

Tying half hitch knots is a great way to cover a jump rings as in this project as well as the belt project on page 82. Half hitch works with all types of materials and can be used to cover just about anything. You can cover up something not so attractive or create your own shapes with wire that can then be covered with leather, linen or whatever suits your project. Half hitch knots do naturally twist as you knot them so you must constantly adjust the knots to prevent it from happening.

WIRE-WRAPPED NECKLACE AND EARRINGS

The rock quartz beads in this project spoke to me when I bought them. They basically said, "Buy me!" but I wasn't quite sure what I'd end up using them in. When the beads found themselves nestled among some amazonite beads in my stash, that's when I knew I had to macramé these beads with wire. Of course, a necklace would need earrings to complete the pretty set. You will need your fancy handmade clasp and ear wires and wire wrapping skills for this project.

Mod Knots

Necklace

square knot (see page 17)

wire wrapping
(see page 25)

Earrings

square knot
(see page 17)

Mod Materials

Necklace

9 8" (20cm) lengths 22-gauge
sterling silver wire

4 2" (5cm) lengths 20-gauge
sterling silver wire

2 4" (10cm) lengths
medium weight
sterling silver chain

4 rock quartz oval beads

7 medium
amazonite rondelles

10 tiny amazonite rondelles

2 round swirl bone beads

2 extra small round
bone beads

fancy hook clasp (see page 26)

macramé board

T-pins

masking tape

round-nose pliers

chain-nose pliers

metal file

wire cutters

Earrings

6 6" (15cm) lengths 22-
gauge sterling silver wire

2 sterling silver ball
ended headpins

4 rock quartz oval beads

2 medium
amazonite rondelles

4 tiny amazonite beads

2 extra small round bone
beads

pair of fancy handmade
ear wires (see page 26)

round-nose pliers

chain-nose pliers

wire cutters

Necklace

1. CREATE WIRE WRAPPED LOOP TO START THE NECKLACE
Start with the center section of the necklace: Take 3 8"
(20cm) lengths of 22-gauge sterling silver wire, hold them
together tightly and wire wrap a closed loop. Trim any excess
wire and file any sharp ends.

2. SECURE TO BOARD AND ADD BEADS
Pin the wire to the board through the loop. Make sure it's
nice and secure. Thread on an extra small bone bead, an
amazonite rondelle and a rock quartz bead to the filler wire,
then secure it to the board with tape.

3. TIE WIRE KNOT AND TIGHTEN WITH PLIERS
Begin a square knot by tying a half knot. Grasp each
knotting wire with a pair of pliers and pull gently but
firmly to tighten the knot, being very careful not to
leave marks on the wire. See how the wire nicely
frames the beads.

4. COMPLETE FIRST SQUARE KNOT
Finish the other half of the square knot and again
pull with pliers to tighten the knot.

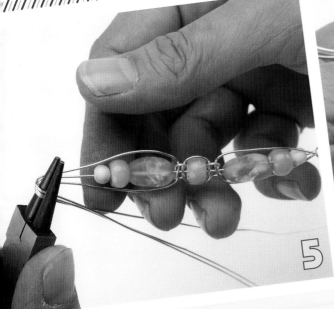

5. CONTINUE ADDING BEADS AND KNOTTING

Thread onto the filler wire another amazonite bead and then tie another square knot, always using pliers to aid you with the wire. Add another quartz, an amazonite and the other bone bead. Remove the section from the board and wrap a loop with the remaining wire.

6. WIRE WRAP LOOP TO FINISH NECKLACE SEGMENT

Complete the loop by grasping it carefully with the round-nose pliers and wrapping the tail around a couple of times. Trim any excess wire and adjust the loop. Make sure all 3 strands of wire are flat and the loop looks attractive. There should be no exposed sharp points on the wire ends. File the ends if necessary to smooth them. This piece will serve as the center segment of your necklace.

7. START NEW SEGMENT CONNECTED TO CENTERPIECE

Begin your next section with a loop made from another 3 8" (20cm) strands of 22-gauge wire. Thread the loop onto the completed section and then wire wrap that loop closed. Trim any excess wire and file any sharp ends.

8. BEGIN BEADING AND KNOTTING PATTERN

Pin the necklace parts to the board at the new loop as shown. Thread a tiny amazonite bead onto the filler wire, tape that wire down and tie a square knot with the others. Carefully use your pliers to pull the knot tight.

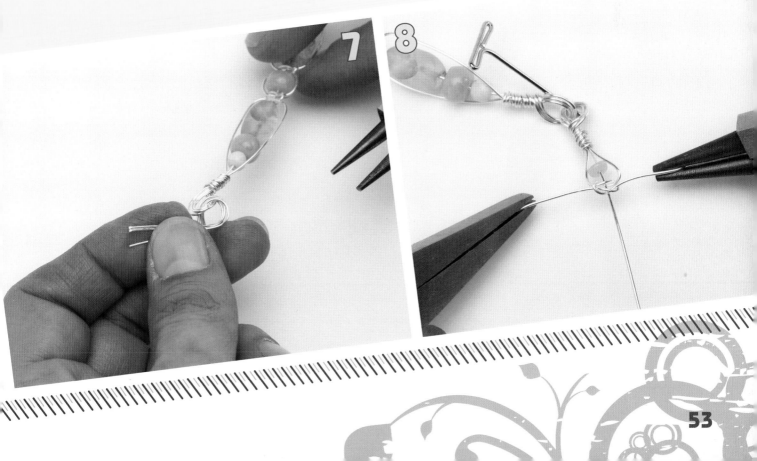

9. COMPLETE THIS SECTION AND REPEAT ON OTHER SIDE
Follow this sequence: quartz bead, square knot, tiny amazonite bead, swirl bone bead, tiny bead, square knot. Add a medium amazonite rondelle onto the filler wire (removing the tape to thread it on, then replacing the tape) and tie a square knot. Add a tiny amazonite bead and wire wrap a closed loop. Trim the excess wires and smooth the ends. Repeat steps 8 and 9 for the other side of the necklace.

10. WRAP A LOOP TO CONNECT THE PARTS
Using one of the shorter lengths of 20-gauge silver wire, wrap a loop and thread it onto the loop at either end of the necklace. This will help attach chain to the back of the necklace. Close the loop.

11. ADD CHAIN TO NEW LINK
Add an amazonite bead and wrap a loop. Thread a piece of chain onto the loop and then wrap the loop shut.

12. ATTACH CLASP WITH LINK
At the end of the length of chain, repeat the wire wrap link this time using a tiny amazonite bead. Wrap the final loop and thread on the clasp. Close the loop.

13. ADD CHAIN AND FINISH NECKLACE
Repeat the steps to attach the chain and clasp to the other side of the necklace. When the final loop is wrapped, make it a bit larger and close it. The hook will attach here.

14 **15**

amazonite bead onto a sterling silver headpin. Make a loop and thread the headpin onto the loop of the top section of the earring and then close the loop. Trim any excess wire. Repeat for the other earring.

Earrings

14. CREATE BEAD DANGLE

The earrings are made up of two sections. The top section is like a section of the necklace. The other section is a dangle made with a headpin. Start the macramé section by wire wrapping a loop with the 3 strands of wire to a jump ring. Pin the ring and wires to the macramé board and thread a bone bead, then an amazonite rondelle onto the filler wire. Tape the filler down and tie a square knot around it. Add a quartz bead to the filler and tie another square knot around it. Add a tiny amazonite bead and finish this section with a closed wire wrapped loop. Thread a quartz bead and an

15. ATTACH EAR WIRES

When the earrings are complete, attach them to ear wires—either those you've made yourself (see page 26), as shown here, or store-bought findings—by opening up the loop on the ear wire and slipping the jump ring into it. Make sure the ear ring is facing the correct direction. Close the loop on the ear wire. Repeat with the other earring.

Variation: Chunky Amethyst With Suede

The variation of this necklace employs the same knots, just different materials. What's different about this necklace is the use of suede and waxed linen with chunky beads. The amethyst beads had holes that could not accommodate the suede, but I really wanted to find a way to combine the two in a project. By using waxed linen to string through the beads, I found I could make it work. The suede and linen were first tied to a wire-wrapped loop, and that loop was later connected to the chain. The beads were strung onto the linen and the suede tied around the beads. Large silver caps were used to camouflage the connection. This necklace is finished the same way as the quartz and amazonite necklace.

TURQUOISE DONUT AND WIRE BRACELET

Donut beads are used in macramé all the time. They're perfect for having materials mounted with a lark's head knot to them. Donuts are available in many types of materials and sizes, but I like turquoise the best. This bracelet combines small donuts with wire macramé and some really interesting glass beads, and the results are so cool.

Mod Knots

lark's head knot (see page 15)

square knot (see page 17)

repeating half knot sennit
(see page 17)

alternating square knot
(see page 19)

Mod Materials

6 14" (36cm) lengths
26-gauge sterling silver wire

10 24" (61cm) lengths
26-gauge sterling silver wire

2 small turquoise donut beads

2 small barrel raku glass beads

3 extra small raku glass beads

1 extra small turquoise nugget

4 large jump rings or chain links

1 lobster claw clasp

macramé board

T-pins

masking tape

round-nose pliers

chain-nose pliers

wire cutters

metal file

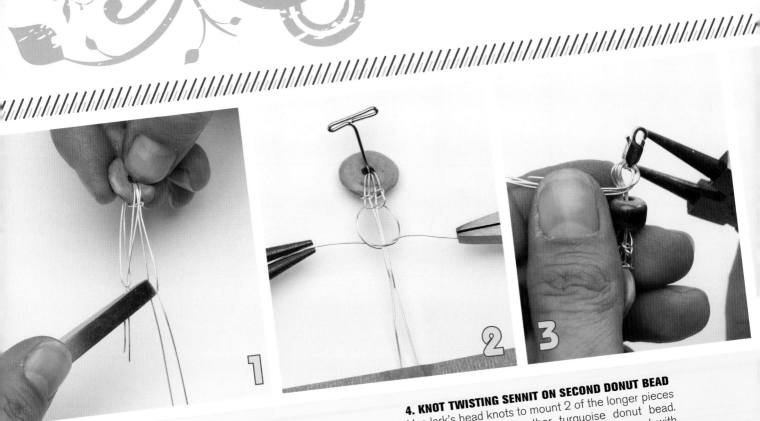

1. ATTACH WIRE TO DONUT BEAD
Use lark's head knots to mount 2 pieces of the shorter silver wire to a turquoise donut bead. Pull the wires tight with chain-nose pliers.

2. SECURE TO BOARD AND TIE KNOT
Attach the donut to the macramé board with a T-pin and tape down 2 filler wires. Tie a square knot with 1 and 4 using the pliers to gently pull the knot tight.

3. ADD GLASS BEAD AND CLASP
Thread a glass bead onto all 4 wires, and wrap a loop. Thread a lobster claw clasp onto the loop and wrap the loop closed. Trim any excess wire and file any sharp ends.

4. KNOT TWISTING SENNIT ON SECOND DONUT BEAD
Use lark's head knots to mount 2 of the longer pieces of silver wire to the other turquoise donut bead. Secure the donut bead to the macramé board with T-pins and tie a sennit of 10 repeated half knots.

5. ATTACH SECTIONS WITH WIRE-WRAPPED LOOP
Use the round-nose pliers to wrap a rather large loop with the wires and thread on the other turquoise donut. Make sure there's enough room in the loop to accommodate the size of the donut. Wrap the loop closed and trim away excess wire.

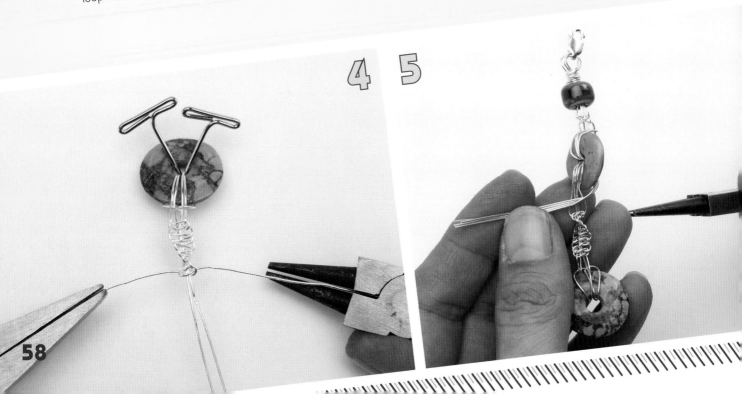

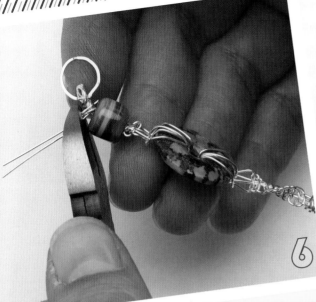

6

7

6. MOUNT NEW SECTION TO OPPOSITE SIDE OF DONUT
Use lark's head knots to mount 2 pieces of the shorter wire to the turquoise donut that the twisting knot is on. Pin the piece to the board and tie a square knot. Remove the piece from the board and thread a glass bead onto all 4 wires. Wrap a loop with the wires and thread a jump ring onto the loop. Close the loop with a couple of wire wraps. Trim any excess wire and file any sharp ends.

7. CREATE ALTERNATING SQUARE KNOT SECTION
To start the next section, take 4 strands of the longer pieces of wire and mount them onto a jump ring with lark's head knots. Secure the jump ring to the board with T-pins. Divide the 8 wire strands into 2 sections of 4. Tape down wires 2 and 3 and 6 and 7 and tie 2 square knots, side by side, with 1 and 4 and 5 and 8, respectively. Remove the tape. Now secure wires 4 and 5 and tie a square knot with wires 3 and 6 to form a second row. Repeat rows 1 and 2 to form an alternating square knot sequence. Remove the wires from the board, thread a small

glass bead onto all 8 strands and wrap a loop. Thread the jump ring from the last step onto the loop and wrap it closed, trimming any excess wire.

8. REPEAT ALTERNATING SQUARE KNOT SEQUENCE
Repeat step 7 on the other side of the same jump ring. When the small bead is threaded onto the wires, wrap a loop and add a jump ring to the loop. Wrap the loop closed and trim any excess wire.

9. COMPLETE BRACELET
The last section of this bracelet uses 2 of the shorter pieces of wire connected to the last jump ring with a lark's head knot. Tie a half knot to start a square knot. Thread the small turquoise bead and a small glass bead onto the filler wires. Complete the square knot. Wire wrap a loop and thread on the last jump ring. This is what the lobster claw clasp attaches to to close the bracelet. Close the loop and trim any excess wire.

8

9

PEARL CHANDELIER EARRINGS

The macramé almost disappears in these chandelier earrings. As the wire creates a lace-like effect that frames the beads perfectly, the design becomes all about the bead choices. In this case, I've opted for pearls and iolite, but this project works well with many varieties of pearls and semiprecious beads (you might try mixing up your choice of wire, too!). Dangles add movement and fluidity.

Mod Knots

lark's head knot
(see page 15)

alternating square knot
(see page 19)

Mod Materials

2 2¼" (6cm) lengths 16-gauge sterling silver wire

12 12" (30cm) lengths 26-gauge sterling silver wire

2 2" (5cm) lengths 22-gauge sterling silver wire

30 26-gauge sterling silver headpins

54 small freshwater pearls

24 extra small faceted iolite beads

pair of fancy handmade ear wires (see page 26)

macramé board

T-pins

masking tape

round-nose pliers

chain-nose pliers

wire cutters

hammer

bench block or anvil

1. FORM TWO IDENTICAL EARRING FRAMES

Take both lengths of 2¼" (6cm) 16-gauge wire and hammer the tip of each end flat. Use your fingers to bend one of the pieces slightly in the middle, and then use round-nose pliers to roll up each of its flattened ends into curls. Repeat with the other piece of wire to create an identical frame to ensure the earrings match.

2. MOUNT WIRES TO FRAME

Pin one of the wire frames to the macramé board. Take 6 of the 12" (30cm) lengths of 26-gauge wire and attach each one to the frame, one at a time, with lark's head knots. Pull each knot tight with chain-nose pliers. You should now have 12 wire strands, 6 on each side of the wire frame.

3. ADD PEARLS AND BEGIN KNOTTING

Position wires 1–4 and 8–12 out of the way, as shown, so you can first work with the others. String 1 pearl onto wire 6 and 1 onto wire 7. Tie strands 5 and 8 in a square knot around these fillers, tightening the knots by pulling gently but firmly with pliers.

4. ESTABLISH ALTERNATING SQUARE KNOT PATTERN

Begin the alternating square knot pattern by positioning wires 3–4 and 8–9 back in your work area. Thread a pearl each onto wires 4, 5, 8 and 9. Tie 3 and 6 in a square knot around 4 and 5, and tie 7 and 10 in a square knot around 8 and 9.

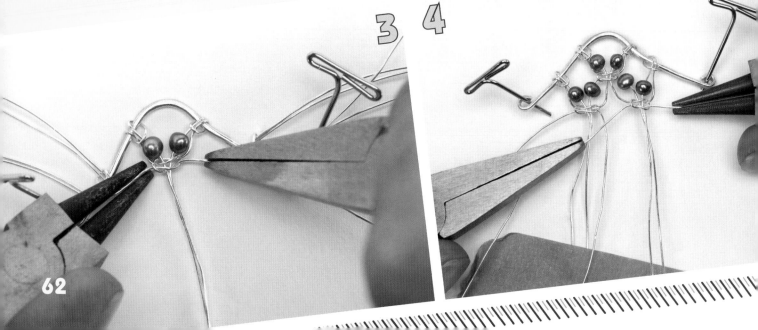

5. WIRE WRAP ENDS INTO LOOPS

Continue tying the alternating square knot pattern until 4 rows have been established. Then, on each of strands 1–3 and 10–12, thread on a freshwater pearl, wire wrap the strand into a small closed loop beneath the pearl and trim any excess wire. For all of the other strands, finish with a small closed wire-wrapped loop.

6. ADD IOLITE DANGLES

Thread an iolite bead onto a headpin. Twist the pin into a loop just above the bead. Thread this into the loop at the bottom of strand 1 and wire wrap it closed to complete the dangle design element. Repeat to add dangles in this order, from left to right: freshwater pearl, iolite, freshwater pearl, iolite, iolite, stack of 4 alternating iolites and freshwater pearls as a center dangle, and then the right side of the earring mirroring the left (iolite, iolite, freshwater pearl, iolite, freshwater pearl, iolite).

7. ADD LINK TO CONNECT EAR WIRE

Add a dangle to each spiral end of the frame created in step 1 by threading first a freshwater pearl and then an iolite bead onto a headpin, twisting the pin into a loop just above the beads and threading the loop through the end of each spiral before securing it with a wire wrap. Finish the earring by cutting a short length of wire, making a wire-wrapped loop at one end, threading on a freshwater pearl, iolite bead and freshwater pearl in that order, and then finishing with a wire-wrapped loop that is threaded through the top of the frame of the earring. Add the ear wire by slightly opening the loop of the ear wire, threading the earring onto it, and closing the ear wire loop. Repeat the process beginning with step 2 to create a second earring, being sure to check your work periodically against the first earring to be sure the two match.

LEATHER POWER CUFF BRACELET

This cuff bracelet is fierce! You almost have to make two so you can have twice the power. It's a variation of a cuff bracelet I designed awhile back for some fashion industry clients. The original cuff was made out of satin rattail, but in modifying my own version, I wanted it in leather. Who wouldn't? So, I incorporated heavyweight silver wire for structure and two extremely cool silver wire coil buttons to secure the cuff.

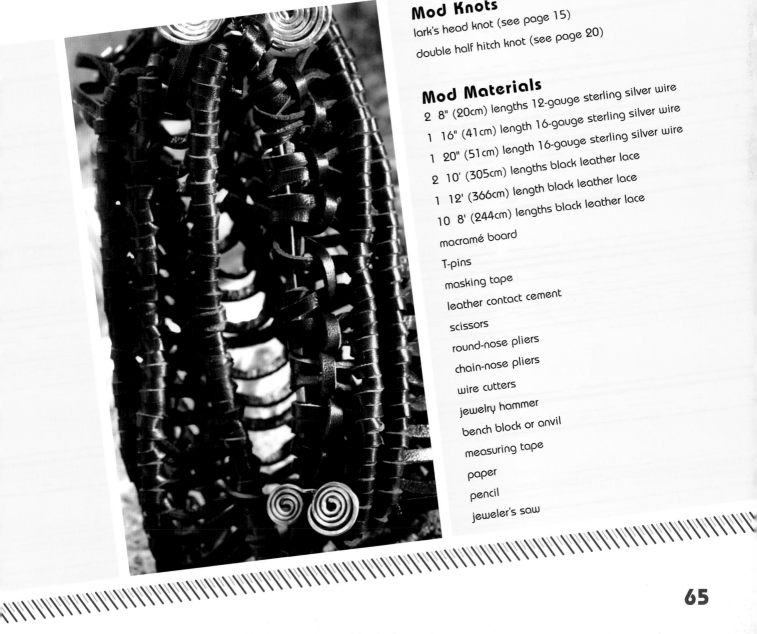

Mod Knots
lark's head knot (see page 15)
double half hitch knot (see page 20)

Mod Materials
2 8" (20cm) lengths 12-gauge sterling silver wire

1 16" (41cm) length 16-gauge sterling silver wire

1 20" (51cm) length 16-gauge sterling silver wire

2 10' (305cm) lengths black leather lace

1 12' (366cm) length black leather lace

10 8' (244cm) lengths black leather lace

macramé board

T-pins

masking tape

leather contact cement

scissors

round-nose pliers

chain-nose pliers

wire cutters

jewelry hammer

bench block or anvil

measuring tape

paper

pencil

jeweler's saw

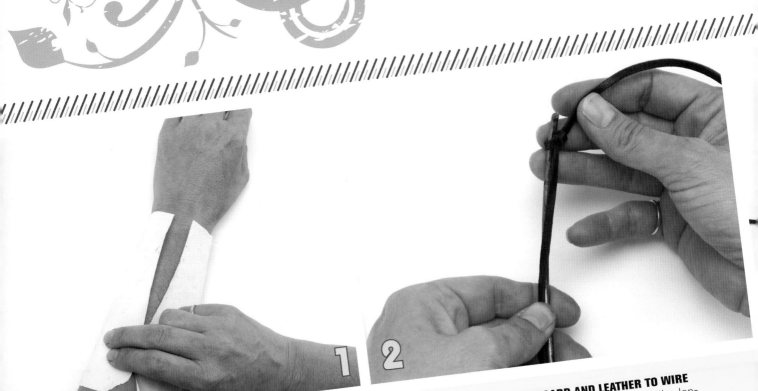

1. CREATE CUFF TEMPLATE
You'll need 2 measurements: The circumference of the wrist of the intended recipient (at the bottom of the wrist where the cuff will rest) and the circumference of the forearm about 7" (18cm) up from the wrist. Transfer those 2 measurements to a piece of paper by drawing 2 centered parallel lines of those lengths 7" (18cm) apart. Connect the lines and then cut the template out. Wrap it around the wrist to test the fit and adjust as necessary.

2. ADD LEATHER STRIPS TO HEAVY WIRE
Tie a short length of leather lace to each of the 8" (20cm) lengths of heavy 12-gauge sterling silver wire. (Note: When first cutting the wire to size, you'll need a jeweler's saw, rather than ordinary wire cutters, to cut such thick wire.) Secure the knots and some of the leather onto the wire with leather contact cement, allow to the cement to dry and trim the ends.

3. MOUNT CUFF TEMPLATE TO BOARD AND LEATHER TO WIRE
Tape your cuff template to your macramé board with the longest edge on the left and one of the diagonals at the top, being careful not to completely conceal the edges of your pattern (you'll need to see them). Tape one of the leather-covered wire pieces from step 2 along the top edge of your pattern. Secure one of the 10' (305cm) pieces of black leather lace to the furthest left position on the top bar with a lark's head knot. Then secure each of the 10 8' (244cm) pieces of lace side by side with lark's head knots across the rest of the bar.

4. BEGIN KNOTTING DIAGONAL DESIGN ELEMENTS
Lay strand 1 across strands 2–22 at a very slight diagonal and secure each strand to it with a double half hitch knot. Strand 1 now becomes strand 22. Again, lay strand 1 (formerly strand 2) across strands 2–22 at a parallel diagonal and secure each strand to it with a double half hitch knot. Again strand 1 becomes strand 22.

5. CONTINUE DOUBLE HALF HITCH KNOTS

Lay strand 22 across strands 1–21 at a slight diagonal (a bit less slight than in the previous step), hold it in place with a T-pin at the edge to help direct the angle, and secure each strand to it with a double half hitch knot, working right to left. Strand 22 now becomes strand 1. Again, lay strand 22 (formerly strand 21) across strands 1–21 at a parallel diagonal and secure each strand to it with a double half hitch knot.

6. SECURE ENDS TO SECOND WIRE

Repeat step 4. Repeat step 5. Repeat step 4. Lay the other piece of leather-covered wire from step 2 across the bottom edge of the pattern and secure each strand to it with a double half hitch knot. Coat all of the knots with leather contact cement, let them dry and trim the ends.

7. HAMMER WIRE FLAT

Take a 16" (41cm) piece of 16-gauge silver-colored wire and twist it into a small loop in the center and hammer it flat and closed.

8. FORM SPIRAL CLOSURE WITH PLIERS

Wind one end of the wire into a spiral, working toward the center of the piece. Working in the opposite direction, wind the other end of the wire into another spiral. Make sure the size is right to fit through the spaces between the rows of knots on the cuff. Hammer the spirals flat to work harden them.

9. CREATE LARGER SPIRAL CLOSURES

Repeat steps 7 and 8 to make another coil button for the cuff, this time beginning with a 20" (51cm) piece of wire to make slightly larger spirals. Use small scraps of leather lace to tie one of these buttons onto each end of the leather-covered wires about 1" (3cm) in from the end.

10. ADJUST FIT AS NECESSARY

Push the ends of the spirals through the slots in the other end of the cuff bracelet to make sure they'll secure it closed. Adjust their positioning if necessary.

INSPIRED ASYMMETRY NECKLACE

Collecting beads has been a passion of mine since childhood. My bead collection has grown so much through the years that sometimes it's like having my very own bead store. Couple that with all of the jewelry-making techniques I've learned along the way, and I believe this necklace is the perfect example of the two passions meeting and greeting. It combines wirework, a diverse array of macramé knots and labradorite beads in different shapes and sizes. Check out the centerpiece! What a bead!

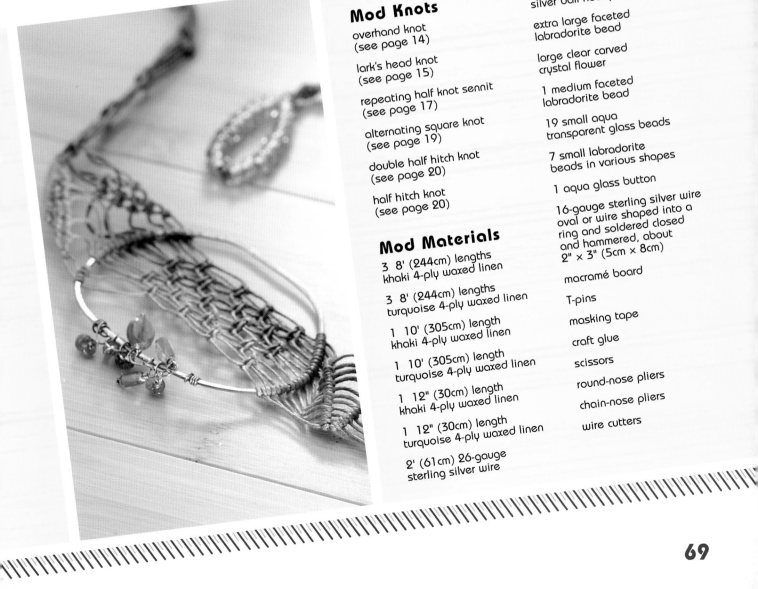

Mod Knots

overhand knot
(see page 14)

lark's head knot
(see page 15)

repeating half knot sennit
(see page 17)

alternating square knot
(see page 19)

double half hitch knot
(see page 20)

half hitch knot
(see page 20)

Mod Materials

3 8' (244cm) lengths
khaki 4-ply waxed linen

3 8' (244cm) lengths
turquoise 4-ply waxed linen

1 10' (305cm) length
khaki 4-ply waxed linen

1 10' (305cm) length
turquoise 4-ply waxed linen

1 12" (30cm) length
khaki 4-ply waxed linen

1 12" (30cm) length
turquoise 4-ply waxed linen

2' (61cm) 26-gauge
sterling silver wire

7 26-gauge sterling
silver ball headpins

extra large faceted
labradorite bead

large clear carved
crystal flower

1 medium faceted
labradorite bead

19 small aqua
transparent glass beads

7 small labradorite
beads in various shapes

1 aqua glass button

16-gauge sterling silver wire
oval or wire shaped into a
ring and soldered closed
and hammered, about
2" × 3" (5cm × 8cm)

macramé board

T-pins

masking tape

craft glue

scissors

round-nose pliers

chain-nose pliers

wire cutters

1. THREAD LINEN THROUGH BEAD AND SECURE KNOT

Use the 2 shortest lengths of waxed linen to thread through the extra large labradorite bead that will serve as the centerpiece of the necklace. Knot the cords tightly with an overhand knot as shown, forming a close fitting loop around the bead, and glue the knot. When the glue is completely dry, trim the ends.

2. ATTACH THREAD FOR BOTH SIDES OF THE NECKLACE

Tape the extra large labradorite bead to your macramé board, with the loop facing toward you. At the right side of the loop, working left to right, attach 3 8' (244cm) khaki strands, then 3 8' (244cm) turquoise strands, one at a time onto the loop, lining the knots up side by side. Working right to left usign lark's head knots, attach the 10' (305cm) pieces of each color of waxed linen side by side onto the left side of the loop as shown.

3. TIE SENNIT AND ATTACH FLOWER BEAD AND GLASS BEAD

Use the 4 strands at the left of the loop to tie a sennit of repeating half knots to form a twist that's about ¾" (2cm) long (about 20 knots). Take strands 2 and 3, thread them through the hole in the center of the flower bead (from the wrong side through to the front) and thread on a small light blue glass bead. Thread them back through the center of the flower—the small bead will act as a stopper and this will serve to thread the flower onto the necklace.

4. CREATE SENNIT AND ADD LABRADORITE BEAD

Begin another series of repeated half knots to form a twist that's about 1" (3cm) long. Thread cords 2 and 3 through the other medium-sized labradorite bead, rejoin them with the other 2 cords on the other side of the bead and begin tying another series of repeated half knots. Make sure the bead sits snugly within the twisting sennits.

5. CONTINUE SENNIT AND CREATE CLASP

Continue until this side of the necklace has reached your desired length. Combine strands 1 and 2 and thread about 9 small blue-tinted glass beads onto them, or until you've formed half a loop that's an appropriate size to slide over the glass button that will serve as the other half of your clasp. Thread the other 9 small aqua transparent glass beads onto strands 3 and 4. Tie all the strands together into a loop with an overhand knot. Coat the knot with a dot of craft glue, let it dry, and trim the ends.

6. CREATE DIAGONAL DESIGN ELEMENTS

Now working on the right side of the necklace, tie 4 linear series of double half hitch knots diagonally back and forth, as outlined on page 20. Pull all of the strands under the top of the oval and then through and over the bottom of the oval, and position the oval about ¾" (2cm) from the last diagonal design element. Tie each of the 12 cords, one at a time, to the oval using double half hitch knots.

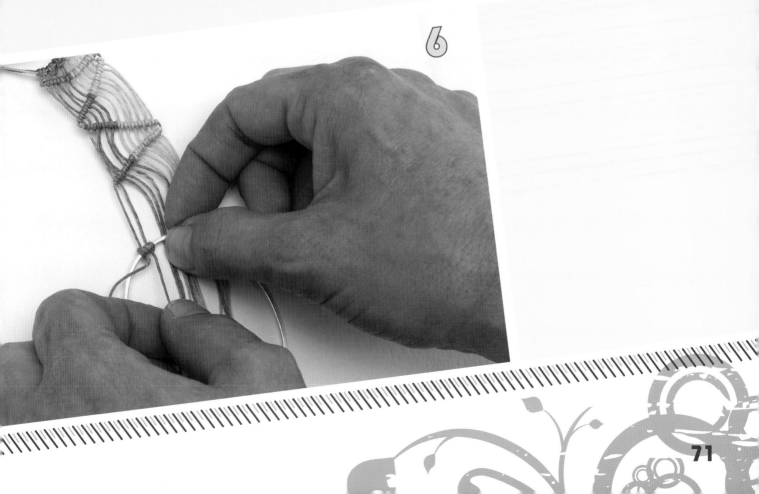

7

7. ESTABLISH SQUARE KNOT PATTERN

Gathering 4 cords at a time, tie 8 rows of a loosely spaced alternating square knot pattern centered within the oval. (For the 1st row, square knot 1 and 4 around 2–3, 5 and 8 around 6–7, and 9 and 12 around 10–11. Then tie 7 additional rows in the alternating square knot pattern.) When you've reached the bottom of the oval, secure each individual cord to the oval using a double half hitch knot.

8. BEGIN JOINING THREADS

Lay strand 1 across strands 2–6 at a steep diagonal and secure each of strands 2–6 individually to it with a double half hitch knot. (These knots should have a bit more space between them then the double half hitch knots tied at the top of the necklace.) Repeat on the other side by laying strand 12 across strands 7–11 at a steep diagonal and securing each of strands 7–11 individually to it with a double half hitch knot.

9. CONTINUE DIAGONAL KNOTS AND COMPLETE WITH SQUARE KNOT

Lay what is now strand 1 (previously strand 2) across strands 2–6 at a diagonal parallel to the one above it and secure each of strands 2–6 to it with a double half hitch knot. Repeat with what is now strand 12 (previously strand 11) across strands 7–11 at a parallel diagonal to the one above it. Repeat this process once more on each side. Gather all the ends about 1" (3cm) below the bottom tips of the diagonal design elements in a large square knot, tying a double thickness of strands 1–2 and 11–12 around all the rest.

8

9

10

tip

Some beads available have holes that may not be large enough to accommodate your knotting material, so it's a good idea to bring samples of your cords with you when shopping for beads. If you just have to have something that has an insufficient hole size, you may have to enlarge it. A bead reamer, also available at your local bead or craft stores, attached to a handheld power tool, may do the trick.

Sometimes it's necessary to drill a larger hole using a cordless power tool and a ¼" (6 mm) diamond hole saw drill bit in a small metal dish of water. The water keeps the crystal and the drill bit from getting too hot. Work slowly and be patient—it's a slow and steady process.

10. COMPLETE AND ADD CLASP

Finish this side of the necklace with a series of these chunky square knots spaced about 1" (3cm) apart until you've reached a length even with the other side. Tie on the button to complete the clasp. Glue the knot, let it dry and trim the ends.

11. BEGIN DECORATIVE WIRE ELEMENT

With the 2' (61cm) length of 26-gauge silver-colored wire, start on the broad, outer edge of the large hoop portion of your necklace. Loop the end of the wire around the edge of the loop, leaving a small bit of a tail, and wrap the wire around the tail a few times to secure it to the loop. Tie the wire around the loop a with 8 half hitch knots. Wrap the wire tightly around the loop a few times at the end to secure it before trimming the ends.

12. ADD BEADS TO HOOP

Thread each of the 7 labradorite beads of assorted small sizes onto a headpin and use your pliers to wrap the top of each headpin into a loop. Thread each one onto the outer edge of the wire coil created in the previous step before closing each loop with a secure wire wrap and trimming all the ends.

11

12

METAL CLAY JOSEPHINE BRACELET

My favorite single knot in macramé is the Josephine Knot. It's more complicated to tie than the others, and it's purely decorative. I love the look of the knot when tied with rattail cord. If only it looked like that in metal. I've tried to work wire into the shape with no success. So after much contemplation, I decided to translate the knot into metal with metal clay. Metal clay is a malleable clay that is made up of microscopic particles of pure silver and organic materials. It can be molded and manipulated into many different shapes and forms. Here it takes the form of a Josephine knot using simple materials and cool tools.

About Metal Clay

Metal clay is a malleable clay that is made up of microscopic particles of pure precious metal (in this case, silver) and organic materials. It can be molded and manipulated into many different shapes and forms, decorated with textures and even embellished with lab-created stones or glass. (Everything you can do with it is far too extensive to cover in the pages of this book, but if you enjoy this project, I encourage you to explore it more on your own!) Once dry it's either fired in a kiln or—if the piece is small enough, like this one—fired by hand with a butane torch. In the firing process the organic binders burn off, the piece shrinks slightly and you're left with a piece of solid fine silver.

Most quality bead and jewelry supply stores and many online retailers carry metal clay, but be aware that there are a couple of different manufacturers and the two types are not compatible, meaning they can't be combined. Metal clay has a tendency to dry out quickly if not properly handled, so you may want to first practice your designs with polymer clay, which has similar malleability but is less expensive and more readily available. Always study the manufacturer's instructions before working with polymer or metal clay.

Mod Knots

Josephine knot (see page 22)

Mod Materials

small amount of satin #2 rattail cord for the knot template

enough polymer clay to fit the rattail knot for the mold

low-fire silver metal clay

2 medium amber dichroic glass beads

2 extra small amber dichroic glass beads

2 sections approximately 1½" (4cm) long sterling silver, heavy weight link chain

4 4" (10cm) 20g sterling silver wire

sterling silver toggle clasp

set of 2 stacked playing cards (three cards thick)

olive oil

water

silver/black patina solution

cotton swab

steel wool

round-nose pliers

chain-nose pliers

wire cutters

craft knife

emery board or small pieces of sandpaper in different grades

brayer or small roller or piece of pvc pipe (about 6" [15cm])

fire brick and tripod and metal screen

metal clay work surface

toaster oven for polymer clay

butane torch and butane

Dremel tool with wire bristle brush attachment

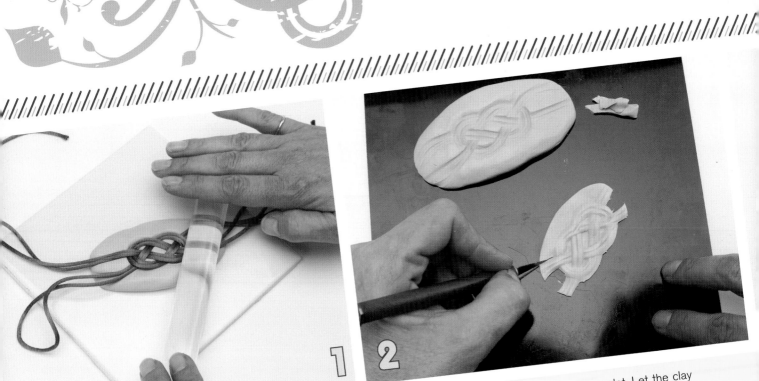

1. TIE JOSEPHINE KNOT FOR MOLD

Tie a large Josephine knot that will serve as the template for your mold. I used rattail satin cord, but you can also experiment with other materials for different consistencies. Condition a small amount of polymer clay, roll it out and lay the knot into the clay. Use a rolling pin or brayer to press the knot into the clay to make a good impression for the mold. (If you don't like the impression, simply knead it out and start over until you have a mold you like.) Bake the mold according to the manufacturer's instructions.

2. MOLD METAL CLAY INTO MOLD

Lubricate the work surface, your mold, your hands and your tools that will be used with the metal clay with olive oil. Roll out the metal clay to a three-card thickness large enough to fit the mold, using the card stacks to assist. Press the clay into the mold evenly with a roller or brayer. Remove the clay from the mold and lay it on the lubricated work surface. Trim around the outside edge of the design with a craft knife. Poke holes in the ends where the wires will connect the silver piece to the bracelet. Let the clay dry thoroughly for a few hours. (Use any remaining clay as soon as possible or put it in an airtight container for later use, as it will dry out very quickly.)

3. SMOOTH EDGES BEFORE FIRING

Use an emery board or small piece of sandpaper to smooth the edges of the dry clay before firing the piece. It's very important that the piece be as smooth as possible. Check the holes to make sure they're clean and smooth. There is slight shrinkage when the clay is fired, so make sure the holes are big enough.

4. FIRE CLAY WITH BUTANE TORCH

Using a butane torch and working on a fireproof surface, fire the metal clay according to the manufacturer's instructions. Let it cool, or quench it in water to speed up the cooling process.

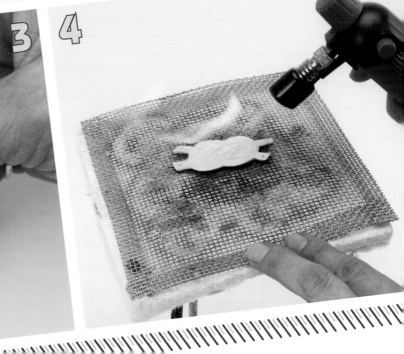

5   **6**

tip

To check if the metal clay is completely dry, slide it across your work surface. If it leaves a moisture trail, it needs more time. If there's no moisture trail, you're ready to do the finish work.

6. ADD PATINA TO SILVER
Use a cotton swab to apply a bit of silver/black solution to the metal clay piece and to your lengths of chain, wire and clasp that will be used in this project. Rinse everything thoroughly with water and dry.

7. BUFF SURFACE WITH STEEL WOOL
Use the steel wool to buff off some of the black patina on the pieces. This leaves the crevices and nooks and crannies dark and gives everything an antiqued feel.

8. ASSEMBLE BRACELET
Begin assembling one side of the bracelet in this order: Wire-wrapped loop, large bead, wire-wrapped loop, chain segment, wire-wrapped loop, small bead, wire-wrapped loop, one half of toggle clasp. Repeat for the other side in the same order.

5. POLISH UNTIL SHINY
The fired metal clay has a white surface to it that needs to be burnished and then polished. Use a Dremel tool with a wire bristle attachment until the white finish has turned completely silver. The more you work the piece the brighter it becomes.

7   **8**

PART 2: ACCESSORIES

If you're anything like me, your passion for personal adornment doesn't stop at jewelry—accessories are just as much fun. Personally, given the choice between the two, I'd find it impossible to decide. So it's lucky I don't have to! In this chapter, you'll find unique macramé projects including everything from belts to bags.

These accessories tend to have simpler designs than the jewelry pieces, but many of them involve more material to manage. The Chunky Wool Fringe Scarf (see page 112) is a perfect example: The entire piece is made by repeating a simple knot pattern, but you'll need to wrestle with extremely long pieces of yarn as you work. (On the plus side, the end result is so impressive your knitting and crochet-savvy friends will hardly believe it's really macramé!) It's a little different working with more strands, longer strands or a combination of both, but all it takes is a little concentration, and you'll find that macramé accessories aren't nearly as difficult to make as they may look.

As with the jewelry section, we'll start simple and then work our way to the more complicated, more time-consuming (but dare I say more awesome) projects—and we'll also stretch the definition of "accessory" to include some novel new ideas. Your iPod will be feeling cozier than ever in the cute Felted iPod Cozy Pouch (see page 102), and the Hemp Yoga Mat Bag (see page 104) will put a kitschy retro spin on your new-age yoga class. Even dog lovers and guitar players will find some special projects in this chapter just for them. Once you've made a few, you will be a certifiable macramaniac, with experience in a wide variety of knotting patterns and design elements.

LEATHER LACE HEADBAND

Do storebought headbands ever give you a pressure headache? Not good. I'm one of those sufferers, but I like the look of headbands, so being the enterprising crafter that I am, I've always made my own. This project uses square knots to tie some great natural leather lace, which will age nicely with time and use. Great stretchy material makes for a comfortable fit. Whoo hoo! It's so simple to make you could create one to match every outfit you own. Plus, this versatile knotting design can be easily adapted to create a bracelet, a belt or even a handcrafted strap for just about anything you can carry.

Mod Knots

square knot
(see page 17)

Mod Materials

7 4' (122cm)
lengths natural
leather lace

2 brown suede
pieces 1" × 2"
(3cm × 5cm)

16–18" (41–46cm)
elastic material

leather contact cement

macramé board

T-pins

masking tape

scissors

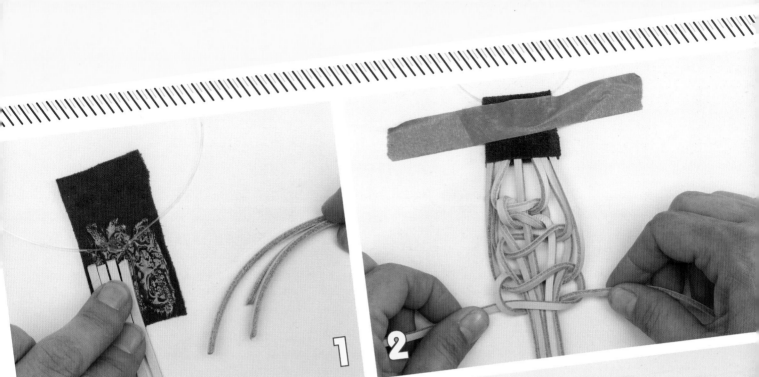

1. ATTACH LEATHER LACE TO SUEDE

Knot the piece of elastic into a loop. Take one of the suede pieces and coat the inside with contact cement. Lay the 7 leather pieces side by side on the glue-coated suede almost to the halfway point, making sure to leave enough suede to fold over the leather pieces. Lay the elastic loop butted up next to the suede, with the knot on the inside so it will be covered in the leather when the suede is folded over. Fold and glue the other side of the suede down to hide the ends.

2. BEGIN KNOTTING SEQUENCE

Secure this piece to your macramé board with a T-pin. Tape the center strand (4) down. Tie strands 3 and 5 into a square knot around 4 to begin the knot sequence. Then establish the pattern in this way: Tape down strands 3–5 and tie strands 2 and 6 in a square knot around them. Next, tape down strands 2–6 and tie strands 1 and 7 in a square knot around them.

3. REPEAT TO DESIRED LENGTH

Repeat this pattern until your headband has reached the desired length. Finish by taping strand 4 down and tying a square knot with 3 and 5 around 4, as you began the piece.

4. TRIM AND GLUE TO FINISH

Leaving about 3–4" (8–10cm) of extra length, trim the ends not to size, but to a more manageable length. Lay some glue onto half of the second suede piece and tape the other end of it down to secure it into place. Position one strand at a time into place and cut it to size, pressing it directly into the glue. Lay the other end of the elastic loop onto the glued area as well, and adhere the other half of the suede flap down to hold everything into place. Allow the headband to dry completely before using. You may want to use something heavy on the suede parts to weigh it down and to hold everything together while the glue dries.

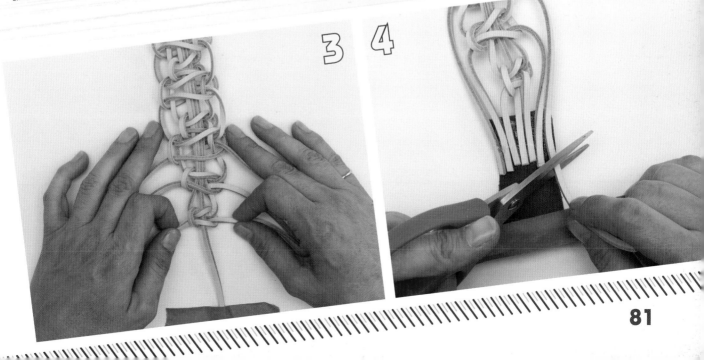

WRAPPED-RING BELT

This project is proof that necessity is the mother of invention. I was putting together an outfit and decided I needed a black belt, but it needed to be the kind that sits on the hips, which I didn't have. Using a large metal ring and the most wonderful black leather lace, I made my own. When I discovered the metal ring was the perfect size but not the most attractive belt buckle, wrapping the ring with leather lace seemed to be the answer. If you find yourself in the same situation, this belt can be whipped up in a flash to suit any outfit—just choose any colors and types of materials you'd like.

Mod Knots
overhand knot
(see page 14)

lark's head knot
(see page 15)

square knot sennit
(see page 18)

repeating half knot sennit
(see page 17)

half hitch knot (see page 20)

Mod Materials
1 6' (183cm) length
black leather lace

2 10' (305cm) lengths
black leather lace

3" (8cm) diameter
metal ring

macramé board

T-pins

masking tape

leather contact
cement

scissors

1. WRAP METAL RING WITH LEATHER LACE

Tie the end of the 6' (183cm) piece of black leather lace to the metal ring with an overhand knot. Glue the knot thoroughly, both to secure it and to adhere it to the surface of the ring. Allow the glue to dry completely. Then, tie the cord in repeated half hitch knots all the way around the ring until it's covered completely. Some of the metal may show through, but that's OK. Be careful your knots don't twist as you work; you may need to pull each one taut and maneuver it into place.

2. ADHERE AND TRIM ENDS

Finish with another dot of contact cement and an overhand knot. Trim the ends flush with the ring after the contact cement is dry.

3. MOUNT LEATHER TO RING TO BEGIN BELT STRAP

Mount the leather-covered ring to the macramé board. Mount the 2 10' (305cm) lengths of leather lace to the ring with lark's head knots, positioning them to cover the spot where the leather ends were glued to the ring—but rather than folding each of the lengths in half, fold each one so the inner cord is 4' (122cm) and the outer cord is 6' (183cm). (This will make your filler cords shorter than your knotting cords and save some material).

4. BEGIN KNOTTING SEQUENCE

Tie a sennit of 3 square knots, each spaced about 1" (3cm) apart.

5. TIE TWISTING SENNIT

Tie a sennit of 8 repeating half knots in one direction, making about 1 complete twist.

6. FINISH BELT BAND

Repeat steps 4 and 5 until you've almost reached the desired length of your belt. Then, repeat step 4 one more time and finish by tying all 4 strands together in an overhand knot. Leave a generous amount of fringe on the end, and trim any excess if desired.

5 6

Variation: **Abalone Ring and Green Deer Leather Lace Belt**

I had the opportunity to have a booth at a bead show in Hawaii a few years back, and as I wandered around to see what the other vendors were selling, I saw an abalone ring that would be perfect for a macramé belt. I had to have it. Glad I bought it. There was also the most luscious deerskin leather lace in teal green. I had to have it too! Glad I bought it too! So here's the result. All I can say is yum! Doesn't it make you want to go out and buy something to wear it with?

BLACK AND BLUE HEART LEATHER BELT

How many times have you been to a bead show or craft store and in the heat of the moment bought the most beautiful beads, only to find out the holes are useless? They've either been drilled crooked or they're too small. It's so frustrating when not even the thinnest materials will comfortably pass through. They may have been strung onto something when they were for sale, but it seems they are never to be strung again. What to do? Here I gave up and found a way to use them in a macramé project anyway: I simply glued them to a heart-shaped belt buckle blank.

Mod Knots

lark's head knot
(see page 15)

repeating half knot sennit
(see page 17)

alternating square knot
(see page 19)

double half hitch knot (see
page 20)

Mod Materials

3 24' (732cm) lengths
black leather lace

1 28' (853cm) length
black leather lace

heart-shaped belt buckle blank,
about 3 3/8" (9cm) wide

approximately 94 faceted
labradorite beads

E-6000 adhesive

macramé board

T-pins

masking tape

leather contact cement

scissors

1. MOUNT LEATHER LACE TO BUCKLE

Secure the buckle face up to the macramé board. Mount the 28' (853cm) piece of leather lace onto the far left of the belt loop with a lark's head knot. Tie each of the other three pieces side by side next to the first with lark's head knots. Lay cord 1 across the others at a slight diagonal, and working left to right, tie each of the other cords with a double half hitch knot around 1. Cord 1 now becomes 8. Lay cord 8 back across the others as shown and tie double half hitch knots from right to left with cords 7–1.

2. TIE A TWISTING KNOT SENNIT

Separate cords 1–2 and 7–8 and set them off to their respective sides so they won't be in the way. Tape down filler cords 4 and 5, and tie a sennit of repeating half knots with 3 and 6 around 4 and 5. Continue the sennit until the twist that forms is at least 2" (5cm) long (about 10 knots).

3. REPEAT STEP 1 AND BEGIN ALTERNATING SQUARE KNOTS

Repeat the process of creating the linear design element outlined in step 1. Then begin an alternating square knot pattern, with the first row being strands 1 and 4 knotted around 2 and 3, and 5 and 8 knotted around 6 and 7. Continue for a total of 5 rows.

4. REPEAT DESIGN ELEMENTS IN PATTERN

Repeat the linear design element outlined in step 1. Repeat step 2. Repeat the linear design element outlined in step 1. Repeat 7 rows of the alternating square knot pattern. Repeat the linear design element outlined in step 1. Repeat step 2, only this time tie the knots using cords 2 and 7 around 3, 4, 5 and 6. This will make a thicker twist. Continue the twist for a length of about 5" (13cm) to create the section shown here.

5. CONTINUE ESTABLISHING BELT DESIGN

Repeat the linear design element outlined in step 1. Repeat 7 rows of the alternating square knot pattern. Repeat the linear design element outlined in step 1. Repeat steps 2 and 3. Repeat the linear design element outlined in step 1. Repeat step 2. Repeat the linear design element outlined in step 1 twice. Coat this final row of knots with the contact cement. Let them dry. Use wire nippers or scissors to cut the ends as close as you can to create a clean end to your belt.

6. GLUE BEADS TO BUCKLE BLANK

Spread E-6000 onto a small portion of the buckle blank near the edge. Begin pressing labradorite beads into the adhesive. Make sure to work in a well-ventilated area.

7. COMPLETE BUCKLE EMBELLISHMENT

Continue in this way, working around the outer rim of the heart first, then continuing with inner rings of beads until the entire buckle is covered. Allow the buckle to dry completely, at least overnight, before wearing the belt.

tip

When you are laying a strand across your working strands and tying the others to it in double half hitch knots, it helps to use T-pins to hold everything in place as you work.

MIXED-MEDIA TIE-SASH BELT

As you go shopping for materials to knot with, try looking for different types of cords that could create interesting effects when knotted together. Experiment with complementary colors in different materials, such as the rust colored rattail and copper leather lace used in this belt project. Combining various materials with different knots can result in pieces with beautifully interwoven textures and colors.

Mod Knots

overhand knot (see page 14)

lark's head knots (see page 15)

square knot (see page 17)

alternating square knot (see page 19)

double half hitch knot (see page 20)

Mod Materials

4 8' (244cm) lengths double worsted 100% cotton yarn, undyed

2 8' (244cm) lengths rust satin #2 rattail cord

4 6' (183cm) lengths double worsted 100% cotton yarn, undyed

4 6' (183cm) lengths rust satin #2 rattail cord

2 8' (244cm) lengths copper colored thin round leather lace

2 8' (244cm) lengths natural colored thin round leather lace

2 large steel rings 3" (8cm) diameter

macramé board

T-pin

masking tape

craft glue

scissors

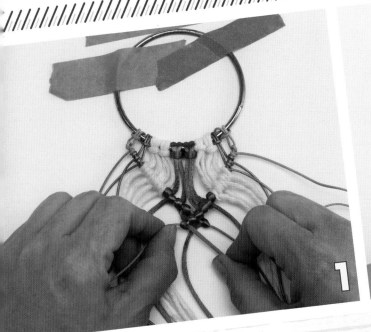

1. MOUNT CORDS AND BEGIN KNOTTED X

Tie the 8' (244cm) lengths of various cords onto one of the large rings with lark's head knots in the order shown. Tape the ring to the macramé board. Cross the first cord (1) and the last cord (20) across one another in an X, with cord 20 on top. Tie cords 2–10, one by one, onto cord 1 of the X using double half-hitch knots. Repeat on the other side with cords 11–19. After the cords cross, continue in the X formation, double half hitch knotting cords 1–10 one at a time onto cord 20, and cords 11–19 one at a time onto cord 1.

2. CONTINUE DIAGONAL DESIGN ELEMENTS

Take strands 10 and 11 and lay them in opposite directions at diagonals over strands 1–9 and 12–20, respectively, at a parallel diagonal to the bottom of the X. Repeat the process of securing each strand to these diagonals with a double half hitch knot.

3. CONTINUE ESTABLISHING DESIGN

Cross strand 10 over 11–20 and strand 11 over 10–1 and lay them at diagonals parallel to those created in step 2. Repeat the process of securing each strand to these diagonals with a double half hitch knot.

4. BEGIN SQUARE KNOT SEQUENCE

Take strands 9–12 and tie 2 square knots. Take strands 5–8 and tie 1 square knot. Take strands 13–16 and tie 1 square knot.

5. ALTERNATE SQUARE KNOT ROWS

Take strands 17–20 and tie 1 square knot. Take strands 1–4 and tie 1 square knot. Take strands 3–6 (all leather cords at this point) and tie 1 square knot. Take strands 15–18 (also all leather cords at this point) and tie 1 square knot. Take strands 7–8 and 13–14 (all yarn at this point) and tie them around 9–12 in a square knot.

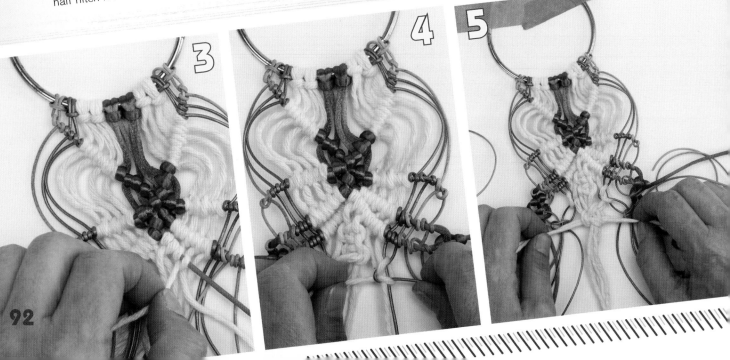

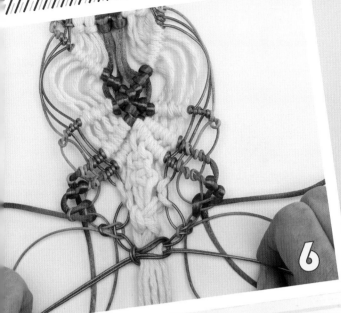

6. ESTABLISH CENTER OF BELT

Take the copper colored cords and tie them around all of the center cords right below the last square knot to form the center point.

7. REPEAT STEPS IN REVERSE ORDER

Repeat steps 5–1, in that order, to create a mirror image of this pattern as the other half of this segment of the belt. Tie off each cord with a double half hitch knot to the second steel ring. Glue all the knots to reinforce them, let them dry, and trim any ends. (Extra glue is a good thing at these connections to make sure the bond is strong.) Glue down any stray ends that may be loose.

8. ADD FRONT SECTION PIECES AND BEGIN KNOTTING

On the opposite side of one of the steel rings of the finished segment of your belt, attach the 6' (183cm) pieces of rattail and the 6' (183cm) pieces of cotton yarn one at

a time with a lark's head knot in the order shown. Tape the ring to your macramé board. Lay strand 1 across strands 2–16 in a horizontal line and tie each strand to this piece using a double half hitch knot. Then take that same strand back across all the other working strands in another horizontal line and repeat the row of double half hitch knots, this time working right to left.

9. FINISH SQUARE KNOT SEQUENCE AND TIE OVERHAND KNOT

Create 1 row of square knots using strands 1–4, 5–8, 9–12 and 13–16. Create a second row of alternating square knots, leaving 1–2 loose and beginning with 3–6, 7–10 and 11–14. Take a double thickness of 1–2 and 7–8 and tie them in a square knot around 3–6. Take a double thickness of 9–10 and 15–16 and tie them in a square knot around 11–14. Take a quadruple thickness of 3–6 and 11–14 in a square knot around 7–10. Finish by tying all the strands in one big overhand knot. Trim the end to the desired length, leaving a generous amount of fringe. Repeat steps 8 and 9, with the ring on the other side of the belt to complete the final segment.

LEATHER AND SUEDE GUITAR STRAP

When I'm living my rock and roll fantasy, I play the bass guitar. So I need a strong, yet hip strap to hold my bass. I've combined macramé leather lace with super sturdy suede hide to create a functional yet stylish strap that will securely carry a heavy guitar. This strap is made using an adjustable strap as a pattern. You need to set the pattern to the size you like and that's how long your fancy strap will be. Your macramé strap won't be adjustable, but it will be really cool!

Mod Knots

square knot (see page 17)

alternating square knot (see page 19)

Mod Materials

adjustable guitar strap to use for a pattern (adjust strap to the desired size)

piece of suede hide at least twice as wide as the pattern guitar strap and a few inches longer on each side

6 8' (244cm) lengths natural leather lace

2 small pieces of heavy weight natural leather hide 5" × 5" (13cm × 13cm)

macramé board

T-pins

masking tape

leather contact cement

self-healing mat

pen

leather hole punch

craft knife

leather scissors

1. CUT SUEDE AND LEATHER FOR STRAP AND END PIECES

Adjust a guitar strap to your desired fit and length. Lay it on the wrong side of a piece of suede and trace it with a pen. Then lay it flush next to the tracing and trace it again. Use scissors to cut around the outside line of the tracing so the suede piece is twice the width of the strap (the pen line down the center will serve as your guide later), leaving a few inches of extra length on each end. Remove one of the leather end pieces from your strap and trace it onto the back side of a piece of leather hide twice, tracing the hole and the slot as well as the outer edge. Cut them out.

2. PREPARE END PIECES TO HOLD STRAP

Protect your work surface with a self-healing mat. Use the leather punch to punch the hole and use a craft knife to cut a slot in each strap piece according to the template. Then, use the craft knife to freehand cut a slot about 1" (3cm) long starting at the base of each hole. (This will help you have the leeway to strap it onto your guitar later.)

3. FOLD AND ADHERE STRAP

Fold the strap in toward the center pen line and glue each side down using the leather contact cement. Place some heavy objects, such as books, on the strap to weigh it down while the contact cement dries for better adhesion.

4. ADHERE ENDS TO STRAP

Thread one end of the suede strap piece through the slot of one end piece, with the right sides of both pieces facing away from you. Glue the flap down to the inside of the strap. Repeat to assemble the other end of the strap. Weigh down the ends and allow the contact cement to dry completely before proceeding.

5. ADHERE LEATHER LACE TO STRAP

Thread each 8' (244cm) strip of leather lace, side by side, through the right side of 1 end piece of the strap (right sides facing out) and glue them down inside the flap. Again weigh down the area just glued and allow it to dry completely.

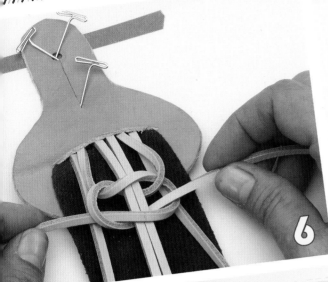

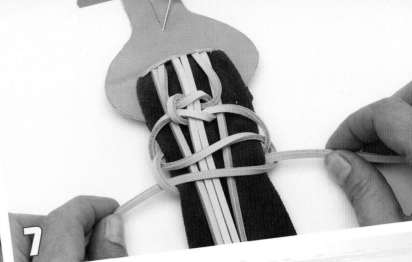

6. SECURE STRAP TO BOARD AND BEGIN KNOTTING

Pin the end piece to your macramé board. Tape down filler cords 3 and 4. Tie 1 square knot with cords 2 and 5.

7. TIE SQUARE KNOT AROUND STRAP AND 4 CORDS

Tape down everything but cords 1 and 6. Use them to tie a square knot around the entire strap as well as the other 4 cords.

8. TIE ALTERNATING SQUARE KNOTS

Tape down strands 2 and 5. Tie a square knot with strands 1 and 3 around 2, and tie a square knot with 4 and 6 around 5. Remove the tape and tape down the middle 2 strands and tie a square knot with strands 2 and 5. Remove the tape and tape down strands 2 and 5 again. Tie 1 square knot with strands 1 and 3 around 2, and one with 4 and 6 around 5. This will be your alternating square knot sequence part of the strap pattern.

9. REPEAT AND CONTINUE PATTERN

Repeat step 7. Then, tape down strands 3 and 4. Use strands 2 and 5 to tie a sennit of three square knots around 3 and 4. Then, repeat step 7 again.

10. COMPLETE STRAP

Repeat steps 6–9 until you reach the full length of your strap. Thread the leather strips through the slot in the leather end piece. Flip the strap over to the wrong side, trim the ends of the strips and use the leather contact cement to glue them down. Again, weigh down the end while the cement dries. Once everything is dry and secure, strap on your guitar and rock!

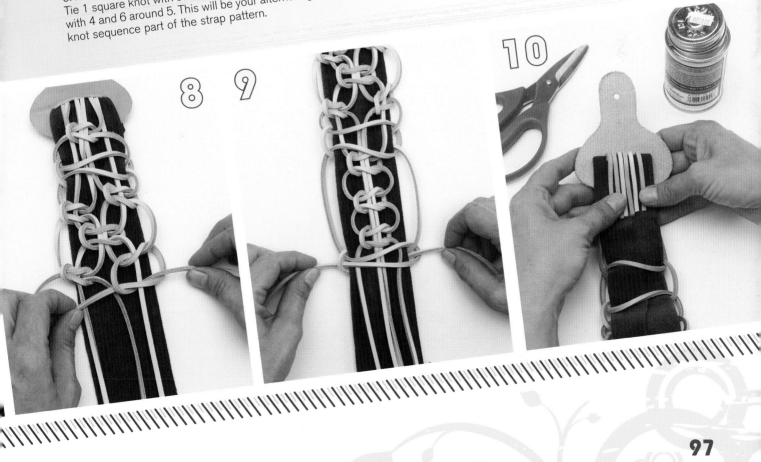

YOUR BEST FRIEND'S COLLAR AND LEASH

I know I'm a dog person. Or maybe I'm a cat person. Can't I be both? I think so. This project can work for either, but dogs seem to appreciate them more, while a cat kind of looks at you like you're crazy. So what else is new? I made this collar-leash combo with a big dog in mind, so I chose a really sturdy polypropylene cord as a base and accented it with thin turquoise leather lace for a little pop of color. Use a collar and leash that fits your dog well to calculate the lengths and also the hardware placement for this project.

Mod Knots

Collar

square knot
(see page 17)

square knot sennit
(see page 18)

Leash

lark's head knot
(see page 15)

square knot
(see page 17)

repeating half
knot sennit
(see page 17)

square knot sennit
(see page 18)

Mod Materials

Collar

2 8' (244cm) lengths
brown poly cord

2 8' (244cm) lengths
thin turquoise leather lace

small metal buckle

small D-ring

macramé board

T-pins

blue tape

craft glue

scissors

Leash

2 20' (610cm) lengths
brown poly cord

2 20' (610cm)
lengths thin
turquoise leather lace

metal clip

macramé board

T-pins

blue tape

craft glue

scissors

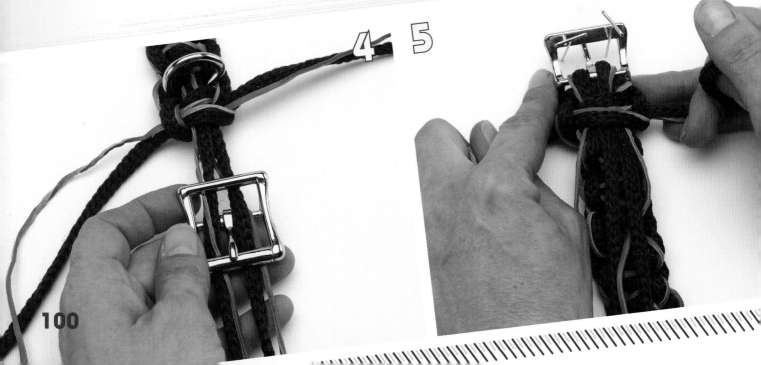

Dog Collar

1. SECURE CORDS AS SHOWN
Measure a collar that fits your pet. Pin the cords to the macramé board as shown. They should be mounted so that the filler cords are just a bit longer than what the collar's finished length should be, with the remainder of the length distributed to the knotting cords. The poly cord and the leather are mounted together because you'll be knotting them together, treating them as double thickness cords.

2. TIE SQUARE KNOT SENNIT
Knot a sennit of square knots to about ¾ of the desired length of your finished collar. If your collar is 15" (38cm) long, knot about a 10½" (20cm) long sennit.

3. ADD D-RING
Add a D-ring to the collar by sliding it onto the filler cords flat side down and tying a square knot to secure it.

4. ADD BUCKLE
Slide on the buckle as shown, threading the filler cords through the buckle and positioning the buckle prong between the fillers.

5. COMPLETE COLLAR
Remove the collar from the board and flip it over. Pin it back onto the board at the buckle and secure filler cords. Tie a square knot to secure the buckle into place. Glue the knot really well, making sure to get the adhesive all around the cords and in between the knots. Allow the glue to dry completely and then trim the ends.

Dog Leash

1. MOUNT CORDS TO LEASH CLIP

Mount the 20' (610cm) pieces of brown poly cord and thin turquoise leather lace to the leash clip, positioning them so the inner, filler cords are about 4' (122cm) long and the outer, knotting cords are about 16' (488cm) long before securing each strand with a lark's head knot. Bobbin the extra-long cords by tying them with some contrasting scrap cord.

2. BEGIN TWISTING SENNIT

Pin the leash clip to the macramé board and begin tying a very long sennit of repeating half knots until you've reached your desired length for the leash (not including the handle).

3. BEGIN HANDLE

Begin the handle by tying a sennit of square knots. Continue for just over twice what you would like the handle's length to be. Then, flip it over and tie a square knot to secure it to the body of the leash. Tie another square knot for good measure. Glue both knots really well, making sure to apply adhesive all over the cords and in between the knots.

4. TRIM EXCESS

Once the glue has dried completely, trim the excess cords close to the knot. Go get your dog and go for a walk!

FELTED IPOD COZY POUCH

This cute little bag is made by combining macramé with felting, a technique that is very popular with knitters. Felting is the process of making an oversized wool item with the intention of washing and drying the fibers on high heat settings to compress and tighten them, giving the material a completely different, textural look. This bag begins with beautiful variegated Italian wool, and the felting process blends the colors for a unique look.

Mod Knots

overhand knot (see page 14)

lark's head knot (see page 15)

square knot pattern with alternating knotters and fillers (see page 23)

alternating square knot (see page 19)

Mod Materials

This pouch was made from an 85 yd [78m] spool of Italian merino wool yarn by Needful Yarns in purple [color #308 lot 32].)

1 piece of cardboard cut to twice the size of the desired pouch

1 length of yarn 4 times the width of the cardboard piece

24 4' (122cm) lengths yarn

2 10' (304cm) lengths yarn

glass button

macramé board

T-pin

masking tape

scissors

water

clothes dryer

1. MOUNT YARN TO CARDBOARD FORM

Cut a piece of cardboard to a size twice as big as the diameter of your desired pouch. Cut a short length of yarn, wrap it twice around your cardboard and tie it in an overhand knot. One at a time, use lark's head knots to tie 12 of the 4' (122cm) yarn strands onto the mounted piece of yarn on one side of the cardboard. Flip the cardboard over and mount the other 12 pieces to that side in the same way.

2. BEGIN ALTERNATING SQUARE KNOTS

Tie a row of square knots with each set of 4 cords working left to right across one side of the pouch. Flip it over and repeat on the back. Work the next row in an alternating square knot pattern, beginning with strands 3–6. When you reach each edge, combine the final 2 cords in a square knot with the first 2 cords on the opposite side of the cardboard to attach the sides.

3. CONTINUE TO DESIRED LENGTH

Continue until the pouch has reached the desired length.

4. TIE BOTTOM OF POUCH TOGETHER

Remove the piece from the cardboard, turn it inside out, and slide it back onto the cardboard. Begin tying the bottom closed, working from one end to the other, tying pairs of strands that are opposite one another together with 2 half knots in the same direction.

5. ADD STRAP AND FELT POUCH

Once the bottom is closed, trim the ends, but not too close. (When it shrinks you don't want the knots to unravel.) With an overhand knot, attach both 10' (304cm) lengths of yarn to the rim of the pouch where the overhand knot is. Pin this to the macramé board and tie a sennit of square knots with alternating fillers and knotters until you've reached the desired length for the strap. Overhand knot the ends to the opposite side of the pouch. Trim the excess, again leaving a bit extra to compensate for shrinking. Felt the pouch by wetting it and putting it in the drier. Once it's the desired size, shape and density, remove it from the dryer and trim any remaining ends.

Tip

This pouch is made oversized to compensate for the natural shrinking that occurs during the felting process. If you want to customize the size for your pouch for your own mobile device, start with the cardboard template described in step 1. Then, while the pouch is in the drying process, monitor it closely. When it starts shrinking, take it out of the dryer and put the piece of cardboard in it. If it fits, set it aside and air dry the rest of the way. If it's still too big, put it back in the dryer to continue shrinking it. Be sure to check the project regularly so it doesn't shrink too small—once the fibers are felted, there's no going back!

HEMP YOGA MAT BAG

I can't help being one of those people that would rather make something I need than buy it. A holder for my yoga mat is just one of those things. Sturdy hemp makes a good strong frame, and brightly colored leather lace adds a pop of color. (Though you could opt for an entirely hemp project, or use another sturdy cord, like vegan-friendly ultra-suede, in lieu of the leather.) Like the pouch on the previous pages, this project is created by "macramé in the round," working continuously by rotating the piece and knotting the sides together on every other row. Try adapting this approach for bags of all sizes, from tiny amulet holders to big laundry sacks.

Mod Knots

overhand knot (see page 14)

square knot sennit (see page 18)

lark's head knot (see page 15)

repeating half knot sennit (see page 17)

double half hitch knot (see page 20)

Mod Materials

yoga mat

approximately 21 12' (366cm) lengths heavy weight hemp cord, depending on the size of your yoga bag (see steps 2–3)

1 2' (61cm) length orange leather lace

2 4' (122cm) lengths heavy weight hemp cord

2 4' (122cm) lengths orange leather lace

1 8' (244cm) length orange leather lace

1 4' (122cm) length heavy weight hemp cord

metal ring, 2" (5cm) diameter

macramé board

T-pins

masking tape

craft glue

scissors

measuring tape

1. TIE LOOSE SQUARE KNOT SENNIT FOR RIM OF BAG

Gather the ends of the 2' (61cm) length of leather lace and the 2 4' (122cm) lengths of hemp. About 6" (15cm) from the ends, tie the 3 cords together with an overhand knot. Pin the knot to the macramé board and tape down the leather piece as the filler cord. Begin tying a sennit of square knots with the hemp, tying them more loosely than normal. (This will be the rim of the bag, and loose knots create natural spaces to attach the cords that make up the bottom part of the bag in a later step.)

2. USE YOGA MAT AS TEMPLATE FOR BAG SIZE

Roll up your yoga mat and tape it shut with masking tape. Measure the circumference of your rolled up yoga mat. Continue knotting the rim of the bag until it equals this length. Remove the piece from the board and wrap it around the end of your rolled-up yoga mat so that it fits around the mat a bit loosely. Untie your initial overhand knot and knot the ends together in a loop with an overhand knot. Trim the ends, leaving a bit of decorative tassel.

3. MOUNT LENGTHS OF HEMP FOR BAG TO RIM

Count the number of loops in the piece you just created. That's how many 12' (366cm) pieces of hemp twine you'll need to begin the body of the bag. Attach one piece to each loop with a lark's head knot.

4. BEGIN ALTERNATING OVERHAND KNOT PATTERN

Begin a pattern of alternating overhand knots: Start the first row by joining pairs of cords together with an overhand knot. Rotate the bag around as you work around the mat.

5. CONTINUE WORKING IN ALTERNATING PATTERN

Start the second row by taking one strand from each of the previous first 2 pairs and joining those 2 in an overhand knot. Continue joining pairs in that manner in overhand knots for the rest of the row around the mat. Complete 4 rows of alternating overhand knots.

6. ADD HORIZONTAL LEATHER LACE TO DESIGN

Cut a length of orange leather lace to twice the circumference of your mat. Lay it horizontally over your working strands, wrap it around the mat and tie it in a loop with an overhead knot. Glue the knot, allow it to dry and trim the excess. Working in one direction, tie each strand onto the leather strip with a double half hitch knot.

7. COMPLETE BODY OF BAG

Repeat 3 rows of the pattern of alternating overhand knots. Repeat step 6, then repeat 2 additional rows of

the pattern of alternating overhand knots. This should be an ample length for your bag. (If it's not, continue as necessary.) Leave a generous 1" (3cm) or so of length below the last row of knots for added length, and then tie the end of each strand onto the metal ring with a double half hitch knot. Coat these knots with craft glue and let them dry completely before trimming the ends, being careful not to trim them too close to the ring to prevent any strands from pulling loose later with use.

8. CREATE STRAP

Use lark's head knots to attach an 8' (244cm) length of leather lace and a 4' (122cm) piece of hemp to the rim of the bag where the initial overhand knot is. Pin the knot to a macramé board and tape the 2 hemp cords down as your filler cords. Tie a sennit of repeated half knots with the lace, letting the sennit twist as you work. Continue until the handle reaches the bottom orange rung of your bag, and tie all 4 strands of the handle in an overhand knot to that spot. Coat the knot with craft glue, let it dry and trim any excess.

DRAWSTRING LEATHER PURSE

Leather lace is a great material to use for macramé belts and jewelry, but I really love using it for purses. This leather lace is soft and the color is bright and fun. It's the perfect material to use for this little drawstring bag that's just the right size for evenings or weekends, or anytime you simply don't need to carry too much stuff. At the bottom section of the bag, we'll be adding in some extra material, both for a design element and to increase the size. This project translates well to other sizes as well as different materials.

Mod Knots

overhand knot (see page 14)

lark's head knot (see page 15)

alternating square knot (see page 19)

double half hitch knot (see page 20)

square knot pattern with alternating fillers and knotters (see page 23)

Mod Materials

8.5" × 5.5" (22cm × 14cm) piece of cardboard

1 2' (61cm) length turquoise leather lace

1 2' (61cm) length lime green leather lace

24 12' (366cm) lengths turquoise leather lace

12 3' (91cm) lengths lime green leather lace

3 14" (36cm) lengths lime green leather lace

1 10' (305cm) length turquoise leather lace

1 10' (305cm) length lime green leather lace

1 donut bead with a hole big enough for 4 strands of leather to thread through but be snug

macramé board

T-pins

masking tape

leather contact cement

scissors

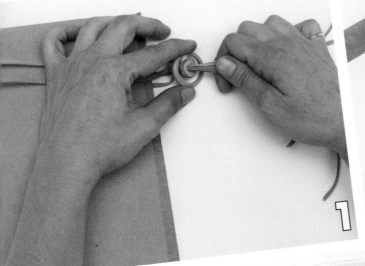

1. CREATE CLOSURE PIECE ON CARDBOARD FORM

Wrap the 2' (61cm) length of turquoise leather lace and the 2' (61cm) length of lime green leather lace around your piece of cardboard. Gather all 4 ends flush together and thread the donut bead onto all 4 ends. The fit of the leather through the hole should be very snug (if it's not, you'll want to select another bead instead). This piece will be your purse's drawstring closure.

2. MOUNT LEATHER CORDS TO DRAWSTRING PIECE

Tie 12 of the 12' (366cm) turquoise leather pieces onto one side of the cardboard with lark's head knots. Flip the cardboard over and tie the other 12 to that side in the same manner.

3. TIE ALTERNATING SQUARE KNOTS AND ADD GREEN CORD

Tie 4 rows of alternating square knots with alternating groups of 4 strands. Take a 14" (36cm) length of lime green leather lace and tie it horizontally around the cardboard over the working strands with an overhand knot at the edge of the cardboard, pushing this piece up against the bottom row of knots. Working from left to right, begin tying each working cord to this horizontal piece with a double half hitch knot. Continue all the way around both sides of the cardboard until every cord has been tied to this piece.

4. KNOT CORDS TO ANOTHER HORIZONTAL PIECE

Take another 14" (36cm) length of lime green leather lace and tie it horizontally around the cardboard over the working strands with an overhand knot at the edge of the cardboard, positioning it about ¾" (2cm) below the row of double half hitch knots. Try to keep the working strands lying flat above this horizontal piece. Working from left to right, begin tying each working cord to this horizontal piece with a double half hitch knot. Continue all the way around both sides of the cardboard until every cord has been tied to this piece,

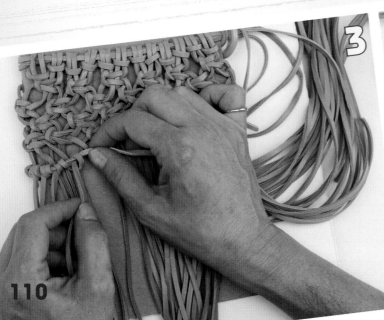

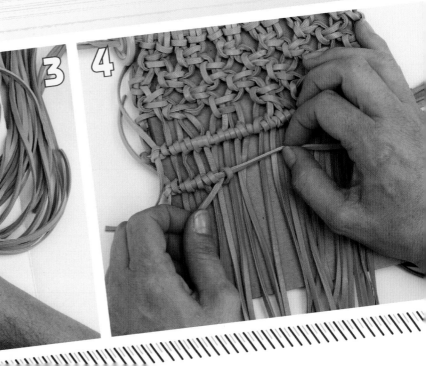

5. ADD SECOND COLOR OF WORKING CORDS

Tie 3 rows of alternating square knots with alternating groups of 4 strands. Again, cut a length of lime green leather lace and tie it horizontally around the cardboard over the working strands with an overhand knot at the edge of the cardboard. Tie each of 4 strands, one at a time, to the horizontal piece with double half hitch knots. Attach a 3' (91cm) piece of lime green leather lace to the horizontal piece of leather with a lark's head knot. Continue in this way, tying four strands in double half hitch knots and then adding a piece of leather lace with a lark's head knot, all the way around this horizontal piece until 12 3' (91cm) lengths of lime green lace have been added.

6. CONTINUE SQUARE KNOTS AND CLOSE BOTTOM OF BAG

Tie 6 rows of alternating square knots. Now that you have introduced a new color of leather with more strands to work with, you'll notice that the base of your purse will be widening. Remove the bag from the cardboard, turn it inside out, and tie the bottom of the purse together with half knots, tying 2 opposite strands at a time, left to right.

Coat all of the knots well with contact cement, including the 3 lime green horizontal pieces of lace at their overhand knots, and let the glue dry completely. Once dry, trim the ends.

7. CREATE MULTICOLORED KNOTTED STRAP

For the strap, take a 10' (305cm) length of blue leather lace and a 10' (305cm) length of green leather lace and, on the bare area of the drawstring piece between the button and the purse, lark's head knot the blue leather onto 2 strands of the drawstring piece and lark's head knot the green leather onto the other 2 strands of the drawstring piece. Pin this to your macramé board and tape down one strand of each color as your filler cords. Begin a sennit of loosely spaced square knots, with about 1" (3cm) in between each knot. Every three knots, reverse the filler cords and the knotting cords, as shown here. This will vary the colors in the strap and help balance material usage.

8. COMPLETE STRAP AND TEST DRAWSTRING

Once the strap has reached the desired length, overhand knot it to the other side of the drawstring piece. Coat the knot with glue and trim. Now you can pull the bead to close the drawstring.

CHUNKY WOOL FRINGE SCARF

I've already mentioned my jealously of knitters and all the beautiful yarns they get to work with. I have to indulge in all of the hand-dyed, gorgeous wools and cottons and all of the other yummy yarns available. If I can't knit them, I'll knot them! I chose some amazing handspun variegated wool yarn for this scarf. You need a lot of material to create such a big project, but trust me, the results are worth the indulgence.

Mod Knots

overhand knot (see page 14)

lark's head knot (see page 15)

alternating square knot (see page 19)

double half hitch knot (see page 20)

Mod Materials

The material used for this project is 4 skeins, 61 yards (56m) each, of 70% merino wool, 20% alpaca, and 10% silk blended chunky variegated wool. The manufacturer is Limarí Multi, hand-dyed in Chile by Araucanía Yarns. This wool will be cut into the pieces mentioned below.

16 18" (46cm) lengths of yarn

14 36' (1097cm) lengths of yarn

14 12" (30cm) lengths yarn

scrap pieces of cord or leather in contrasting color

macramé board

T-pins

masking tape

scissors

Variation:
Green Handspun Wool Scarf

The possibilities seem endless in the different types of yarns you can indulge in. This variation of the scarf uses two different colors of wool. Both are hand-dyed and the teal yarn's texture is variegated; it's both thick and thin. This is a nice contrast to the green yarn, which is uniform in its texture. The yarns for this scarf aren't as chunky, so there are more sections of alternating double square knot. Playing with the color placement of the yarn when it's mounted is another way to design another alternative to these two scarves. Didn't I say the possibilities are endless?

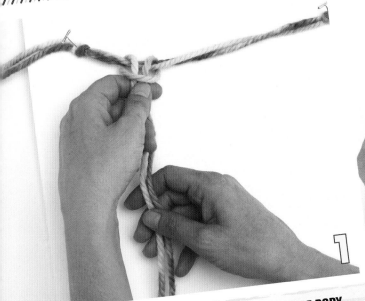

1. PREPARE MOUNTING CORD AND YARN FOR SCARF BODY

Knot 2 short lengths of yarn (about 18" [46cm] each) together at each end to the desired width of your scarf. (Feel free to let the ends dangle; these will blend in with the fringe of the finished piece.) Pin this at each end horizontally across the project. The body of the scarf will consist of 14 separate pieces of yarn 36' (1097cm) each. Preparing this amount of material to knot can be a bit intimidating. 36' (1097cm) is a long piece of yarn and it needs to be handled carefully to keep it from tangling. I find it's best to cut a first piece of yarn and then use that to measure out each additional piece. Mount each piece of yarn to the mounting cord with a lark's head knot as soon as you cut it so the yarn doesn't pile up and tangle.

2. BOBBIN YARN ENDS

Wrap each strand of yarn in a makeshift bobbin to keep it contained and manageable. Here I've chosen scraps in a contrasting color so I can find the ties easily. I've also opted for

leather because it unties easily and won't be intertwined with the plies of the yarn.

3. TIE SEQUENCE OF ALTERNATING DOUBLE SQUARE KNOTS

The knot sequence for the scarf is very simple and will be used for the entire scarf. Feel free to adapt it or tie it up exactly as it is here. Tie a pattern of alternating double square knots for 9 rows. (A double square knot is two consecutive square knots.)

4. ADD HORIZONTAL PIECE AND ATTACH STRANDS

After 9 rows are complete, create another cord identical to the mounting cord in step 1. Double it over, cut it in half and lay the two pieces flush horizontally across the scarf. Tie these 2 pieces together with overhand knot where it overlaps each edge of the scarf. Working left to right, one at a time tie each strand onto the horizontal piece with a double half hitch knot. The fringe of the added cord should come off the sides just like the mounting cord.

5. CONTINUE REPEATING PATTERN TO DESIRED LENGTH
Continue the pattern of 9 rows of alternating double square knots and the added fringe element until the desired length of the scarf is reached. (This one has 6 complete sections.) Finish by adding the final 2 pieces of fringe yarn and tie the last row of double half hitch knots across, left to right.

6. TRIM ENDS TO CREATE FRINGE
Trim any excess yarn at the end of the scarf, leaving at least 6" (15cm) of fringe. Tie groups of 4 strands with an overhand knot to create a decorative fringe, working across the bottom of the scarf. You should have 7 tassels.

7. ADD FRINGE TO OTHER END OF SCARF
At the top of the scarf, add pieces of fringe by tying lark's head knots with the shortest pieces of yarn that were cut. Attach them in between the sections of yarn that were initially mounted to begin this project. Wrap yourself in the luxury of your own hand-knotted wool scarf.

ALOHA BAMBOO HANDLE PURSE

These bamboo handles have a tropical feeling that reminds me of Hawaii. I needed to find just the right material to use to make this bag, and when I saw the cotton yarn—just the color of Hawaiian hibiscus flowers—I knew that was what it needed to be. Combining cool purse handles, soft, pretty yarn and interesting knot combinations, you get an awesome looking bag. I decided to add a suede pouch liner to keep your goodies hidden inside and provide a nice finished look—but your bag would be complete even without it.

Mod Knots
lark's head knot (see page 15)

square knot (see page 17)

square knot sennit (see page 18)

alternating square knot (see page 19)

double half hitch knot (see page 20)

repeating half knot sennit (see page 17)

square knot pattern with alternating fillers and knotters (see page 23)

Mod Materials
8 14' (427cm) lengths of cotton yarn

64 11' (335cm) lengths of cotton yarn

2 bamboo purse handles

macramé board

T-pins

masking tape

craft glue

scissors

Lining (Optional)
Suede hide

leather contact cement

leather hole punch

1. MOUNT YARN ONTO PURSE HANDLE
Tie 4 14' (427cm) lengths of yarn, one by one, in lark's head knots over the horizontal bar of the bamboo handle. Slide two all the way to the left of the handle and two all the way to the right of the handle. Take 32 of the 11' (335cm) lengths and also mount them with lark's head knots between the other four on the handle. Repeat for the second handle. (You may want to tie up the strands in bobbins for easy knotting.) Mount the handle to the macramé board. Put the other handle aside for later.

2. TIE ALTERNATING SQUARE KNOTS
Begin a pattern of alternating knots in this way: For the first row, tie a square knot with strands 1 and 4 around 2 and 3. Continue in this manner with each group of four strands, working from left to right. For the second row, working right to left, set aside strands 1 and 2, now counting the strands from right to left, then tie three alternating half knots with strands 3 and 6 around 4 and 5. Continue in this manner with each group of four strands with two strands leftover at the end. Tie a third row identical to the first row.

3. ADD HORIZONTAL ELEMENT
Lay strand 1 horizontally across all of the other strands and pin it in place. Working left to right, tie each strand individually to this horizontal piece using a double half hitch knot.

4. TIE SQUARE KNOT SENNIT
Take strands 1–4, and tie a sennit of 12 completed square knots. This begins a series of knot sequences across this section of the bag.

5. CONTINUE ESTABLISHING PATTERN
Set aside strands 5–6. Take strands 7–10 and tie a sennit of repeating half knots the same length as the last sennit of square knots. Set aside strands 11–12. With strands 13–16, tie a sennit of four square knots, each spaced about ½" (1cm) apart. Set aside strands 16–17. With strands 18–21, tie a sennit of square knots, switching the filler and knotting cords after each knot. Set aside 22–23.

6. ADD CENTER DIAMOND ELEMENT

Take strand 35 and lay it over strands 34–24 to form the top left diagonal of what will be a diamond shape. Knot each of strands 34–24 to it with a double half hitch knot. Take strand 36 and lay it over strands 37–47 and repeat this process. Set aside the two strands at each end of the diamond formation. Take the four outermost strands from either side and use them to tie a big square knot in the center of what will be the diamond.

7. CONTINUE PATTERN

Complete the bottom of the diamond by taking the strands you tied over in the previous step, laying them inward to complete the diamond shape, and tying each strand to these with a double half hitch knot. Complete the right side of the purse in the mirror image of steps 4 and 5. To do so, simply begin counting the cord at the right edge as strand 1 and follow the instructions to work inward.

8. BEGIN BOTTOM SECTION OF BAG

Lay strand 1 across all the working strands horizontally so that it rests just below the tip of the diamond. Tie every strand to this piece with a double half hitch knot. Starting with a group of strands 1–4, tie a row of double square knots. Then, setting aside strands 1–2 and starting with 3–6, tie a row of single square knots. Repeat step 2.

9. CONTINUE HORIZONTAL ROWS

Lay strand 1 across all the working strands and tie each cord to this piece with double half hitch knots. Lay strand 1 back across the other strands and tie them all to it with double half hitch knots, from right to left. Using the last strand, strand 72, lay that across the others horizontally and tie the others again with double half hitch knots. Bring it back and forth 2 more times so there is a total of 5 coils of double half hitch knots stacked up next to each other.

COMPLETE PURSE AND (OPTIONAL) LINE INSIDE

Repeat steps 2-9 to create the other half of the purse. Line up the bottoms and tie the purse together by tying each strand to its opposite strand with 2 half knots. Glue the knots, let them dry and trim the excess. If you want to line the bag, measure the interior before attaching the sides. Create a template from your measurements for the lining that will be slightly smaller than the inside of the bag, and cut out the material needed. Glue the sides and bottom of the lining together with contact cement. Punch holes 1" (3cm) apart along the sides of the pouch and along the top opening pieces. Place the lining inside the purse and whipstitching the sides of the purse shut, using yarn in a matching color. Sew through the lining every few stitches to secure it. A few inches from the top, tie it off and glue the knot securely. Whipstitch the top portions of the lining to the top of each side of the bag. Glue the knots, let dry and trim the ends.

SUMMERTIME, SUMMERTIME HALTER TOP

I was shopping at my local yarn store when I saw someone knitting the cutest tank top. You already know about my envy of knitters, so, naturally, the challenge to translate macramé into a wearable garment was on, and the Summertime, Summertime Halter Top was born. It's constructed in soft, variegated cotton using alternating square knots. Some are tied tightly and others are tied loosely, and the result is coverage—but not complete coverage. The piece is constructed from two triangles joined together for the bra portion of the top, which is then knotted to a separate empire waist piece. The body of this backless top is pure fringe. Pair this with a cute cami (or, for a more bare look, sew in a neutral-colored bikini top) for a fashion statement to make your knitter friends jealous.

Measuring for the Halter Top

Take the following measurements:

1. Measure yourself around your rib cage just below your breasts to determine the length of strap that is required. This will be for the portion of the halter top that attaches the top and bottom sections together. The strap will be a piece that is created by tying a loose square knot sennit, like the top section made in the Hemp Yoga Mat Bag project on page 104. The loops that form will allow for the sections to attach easily. Add 28" (72cm) to the measurement to accommodate 14" (36cm) straps that tie the top in the back.

2. Measure from the top of your shoulder to just underneath your breast to determine the amount of material needed for the bra sections of the top. Add 14" (36cm) to accommodate the strap that ties behind your neck. The measurement will determine the size of the frame of each bra section. The yarn that fills the bras will be attached to these pieces. You'll need two sections.

3. Measure the distance between the center of your chest bone and your side, under your breast. This measurement will determine the placement of the side sections when they are mounted to the macramé board. The larger the measurement, the further the frame strands will be apart, and the more yarn you'll need to fill the area.

4. The bottom section of the halter top is a loosely knotted flap that has coverage only in the front. To determine the size, you can double the above measurement or just measure yourself around, from one side to the other. And you can always make it wider so it wraps around the back if you'd like. The length of the halter top is up to you but you can measure from under your chest to your hips to get an idea of how much material needs to be used. The knots are tied loosely, so they use less material.

Mod Knots

overhand knot (see page 14)

lark's head knot (see page 15)

square knot (see page 17)

repeating half knot sennit (see page 17)

square knot sennit (see page 18)

alternating square knot (see page 19)

Mod Materials

8 6' (183cm) lengths variegated cotton yarn

3 8' (244cm) lengths variegated cotton yarn

28 4' (122cm) lengths lavender cotton yarn

28 3' (91cm) lengths lavender cotton yarn

16 2' (61cm) lengths lavender cotton yarn

40 8' (244cm) lengths lavender cotton yarn

macramé board

T-pins

masking tape

fabric glue

scissors

measuring tape

3. BEGIN KNOTTING TRIANGLE

Start with the middle 4 strands and very tightly tie a square knot in the center, just below the strap. Gather the left 2 strands of that knot with the 2 strands directly to their left, and tie another square knot here. Repeat to the right of the first knot. Continue in this way to begin a pyramid of square knots.

4. FINISH TRIANGLE PORTIONS

Continue knotting the pyramid until it will completely cover the desired chest area. Repeat steps 1–3 for the other side of the top. Hold it up to yourself to test the fit. If you need to add more coverage, continue tying rows of square knots. You'll notice as you reach the bottom of the section the piece will pucker in the center a little bit; that will help it fit better.

5. CREATE CENTER STRAP

Hold 3 18' (244cm) strands of variegated, coordinating chunky yarn with the ends flush and tie overhand knots about 4" (10cm) apart until you've reached a length of 18" (46cm) (depending on your measurements). Pin the bottom knot to your macramé board and tie a sennit of loosely spaced square knots to a length of approximately 32" (81cm). Then, tie a series of overhand knots about 4" (10cm) apart for another length of about 18" (46cm). This will be the empire waist strap.

1. BEGIN STRAP

Gather the ends of 4 of the 6' (183cm) coordinating pieces of chunky, variegated cotton yarn. Tie them in an overhand knot, leaving about 6" (15m) of fringe at the end and pin that to the macramé board. Tie a sennit of repeated half knots until a 2' (61cm) length is reached for the strap. Repeat to create an identical strap for the other side of the bra portion of the top. Set one aside.

2. MOUNT YARN FOR BIKINI TOP

Take one of the straps from step 1 and split the strands into 2 sections to begin one side of the bra portion. Tape them into a Y on the macramé board. Attach 7 4' (122cm) pieces of lavender yarn on each side, with lark's head knots, at the top of the Y. Attach 7 3' (91cm) pieces of lavender yarn on each side, this time lower on the mounting strands, with lark's head knots. Attach 4 2' (61ccm) lengths of lavender yarn on each side with lark's head knots. Slide the strands up tight on the strap.

6. BEGIN BOTTOM PORTION OF TOP

Tape down the empire waist strap and find the center point. Measure from the center to find the area to cover the measurement you took for this portion of the top. Determine how many square knots are in this area and cut that many pieces of yarn in 8' (244cm) lengths. We're using 40 pieces here. Start at one end and tie each piece onto the bottom loop of the square knot as shown, with lark's head knots across the strap.

7. ESTABLISH ALTERNATING SQUARE KNOT PATTERN

Working from left to right, tie each section of 4 strands in a loose square knot. Don't pull the knots vertically taut; instead, aim to establish a loose, lacy pattern. For the second row, skip the first 2 strands of yarn and then, working left to right, begin tying sections of 4 strands into a loose square knot. Begin the third row identical to the first. Continue tying rows of alternating square knots until the desired length is reached

8. FINISH WITH OVERHAND KNOTS

Once the desired length of the alternating square knot pattern bottom section is reached, tie each four-strand group into an overhand knot 1" (3cm) below the last square knot. Work across the bottom and continue tying overhand knots. Trim away excess yarn. If you want, vary the lengths of the fringe for a different look.

9. PREPARE TO ASSEMBLE TOP

Now it's time to attach the top pieces to the bottom. To make this easier, first trim the strands of each top piece to a more manageable length. Don't trim them completely, though; you'll need some yarn for tying.

10. TIE SECTIONS TOGETHER

Lay the empire waist piece right side down. Find the center point of the empire waist and position the bottom corners of the top triangular pieces so that they meet here. Starting in the center and working outward, attach one of the top pieces by tying the strands, two at a time, into the adjacent top loop of the empire waistband. Repeat to attach the other piece. Coat each knot with fabric glue, let it dry, and then trim the excess.

RESOURCES

Most of the materials and tools used in this book can be found at your favorite local craft retailer. For supplies you can't find locally, contact these manufacturers for more information.

Art Clay World USA
www.artclayworld.com
metal clay supplies

Beadbrains
www.beadbrains.com
www.beadbrains.etsy.com
beads, jewelry and more by yours truly

Eclectic Products
www.eclecticproducts.com
E-6000 adhesive

Eister Glass by Dan Eister
www.daneister.etsy.com
glass beads and Lea Anne
Hartman Designs

Grobet USA
www.grobetusa.com
manufacturer of Griffith
Silver/Black patina solution

MoonDancer
www.moondancer.etsy.com
antiqued brass swallows

Metal Clay Supply
www.pmcsupply.com
metal clay supplies

Rio Grande
www.riogrande.com
jewelry supplies and tools

Soft Flex Company
www.softflexcompany.com
manufacturer of Soft Flex and Soft
Touch wire

Tandy Leather Factory
www.tandyleatherfactory.com
leather craft supplies, including Tanners
Bond Craftsman contact cement

ABOUT THE AUTHOR

Cathi Milligan is long-time designer and craft-of-all-trades kind of gal. A lifelong resident of Los Angeles, she splits most of her time between glassworking and macramé, and she loves to combine the two whenever possible. Other adventures include graphic design, jewelry making, glass fusing, metal clay and, her favorite, glass bead making. She teaches bead making and fusing as well as macramé and other jewelry-making techniques in workshops throughout Southern California.

Cathi has made television appearances on DIY's *Jewelry Making* and *Craft Lab* as well as TLC's *Slice of Life* and Lifetime's *Operation Rescue*. She's written for *Craft:* and *The Flow* magazine, and her jewelry and beads have been featured in *InStyle*, *Bead & Button* and a number of Japanese fashion magazines.

You can find Cathi's jewelry and beads at her Web site, www.beadbrains.com, or at www.beadbrains.etsy.com.

INDEX

GET TIED UP WITH THESE OTHER GREAT F+W MEDIA BOOKS

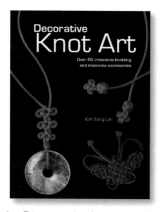

Decorative Knot Craft: Over 20 Innovative Knotting and Macramé Accessories
Kim Sang Lan

Explore the art of decorative knotting to create over twenty imaginative jewellery and accessory projects in Decorative Knot Craft. Eleven exciting knotting techniques are explored, from basic tying techniques to more intricate macrame and ornamental styles. Discover the fascinating history behind knot art; an ancient technique that originated in Korea, traditionally used to decorate clothing and home interiors. Each technique is clearly illustrated with detailed step-by-step instructions and striking photography to ensure you won't be tied up in knots!

ISBN-13: 978-0-7153-2922-1
ISBN-10: 0-7153-2922-7
paperback
128 pages
Z2307

Strands
Jacqueline Myers-Cho

Wonder what would happen if you took a "this" and put it with a "that"? In Strands you'll find the answers lead to nine handcrafted original fabric designs using repurposed or simple materials such as thread, tape, plastic bags, paper and more. Clear step-by-step instructions will show you how to use these innovative creations to craft twenty fashion-forward, easy-to-make projects like wristbands, purses, scarves and hats. Let Strands be your starting point for a journey of discovery.

ISBN-13: 978-1-60061-137-7
ISBN-10: 1-60061-137-0
paperback
128 pages
Z2319

Bead On a Wire
Sharilyn Miller

In her latest book, magazine editor and popular author Sharilyn Miller shows crafters of all levels how to get in on the popularity of jewelry and beading. Inside Bead on a Wire, you'll find an in-depth section on design and construction techniques that make it a snap to get started. You'll love to make the 20 step-by-step bead and wire jewelry projects, including gorgeous earrings, necklaces, brooches and bracelets. You'll be amazed at how easy it is to start making fashionable jewelry that's guaranteed to inspire compliments.

ISBN-13: 978-1-58180-650-2
ISBN-10: 1-58180-650-7
paperback
128 pages
33239

Knit One, Embellish Too
Cosette Cornelius-Bates

Knit One, Embellish Too features warm and cozy knitted accessories for head, hands and neck, all embellished with embroidery, buttons and appliqués. With a little yarn and a little know how, you can quickly create any of the 35+ projects in this book, and author Cosette Cornelius-Bates helps you with both. Learn how to turn a sweater from a thrift shop into a lovely pile of knitting yarn, and then learn the knitting and embellishing techniques to turn yarn into hats, mittens and scarves for yourself and your loved ones. Get inspired to create your own one-of-a-kind knitted accessories!

ISBN-13: 978-1-60061-046-2
ISBN-10: 1-60061-046-3
paperback
128 pages
Z1594

These and other fine North Light Books are available at your local craft retailer, bookstore or online supplier, or visit our Web site at www.mycraftivity.com.